The 4" × 5" Quilt-Block
ANTHOLOGY

182 BLOCKS FOR REPRODUCTION FABRICS

Carol Hopkins and Linda M. Koenig

Martingale
Create with Confidence

The 4" x 5" Quilt-Block Anthology:
182 Blocks for Reproduction Fabrics
© 2017 by Carol Hopkins and Linda M. Koenig

Martingale®
19021 120th Ave. NE, Ste. 102
Bothell, WA 98011-9511 USA
ShopMartingale.com

Printed in China
22 21 20 19 18 17   8 7 6 5 4 3 2 1

Library of Congress Cataloging-in-Publication Data

Names: Hopkins, Carol J., author.

Title: The 4" x 5" quilt-block anthology : 182 blocks for reproduction
    fabrics / Carol Hopkins and Linda M. Koenig.

Other titles: Four inch by five inch quilt block anthology

Description: Bothell, WA : Martingale, 2017.

Identifiers: LCCN 2016042544 (print) | LCCN 2016044147 (ebook)
    | ISBN 9781604688177 | ISBN 9781604688184

Subjects: LCSH: Patchwork--Patterns. | Quilting--Patterns. | Quilts.

Classification: LCC TT835 .H5566 2017 (print) | LCC TT835 (ebook)
    | DDC 746.46/041--dc23

LC record available at https://lccn.loc.gov/2016042544

MISSION STATEMENT

We empower makers who use fabric and yarn
to make life more enjoyable.

CREDITS

**PUBLISHER AND
CHIEF VISIONARY OFFICER**
Jennifer Erbe Keltner

CONTENT DIRECTOR
Karen Costello Soltys

MANAGING EDITOR
Tina Cook

ACQUISITIONS EDITOR
Karen M. Burns

TECHNICAL EDITOR
Angela Ingle

COPY EDITOR
Melissa Bryan

DESIGN MANAGER
Adrienne Smitke

**COVER AND
INTERIOR DESIGNER**
Regina Girard

PHOTOGRAPHER
Brent Kane

ILLUSTRATOR
Sandy Huffaker

DEDICATION

*To our families and quilting friends,
whose gifts of love and encouragement we cherish.*

Contents

6 ✦ Introduction

7 ✦ Selecting Fabrics

8 ✦ How to Use This Book

Block Instructions

10 ✦ Block 1: Raspberries

11 ✦ Block 2: Chutes and Ladders

12 ✦ Block 3: Oh-Oh!

13 ✦ Block 4: Reflections

14 ✦ Block 5: Quiver

15 ✦ Block 6: Bars

16 ✦ Block 7: Thread

17 ✦ Block 8: Preposition

18 ✦ Block 9: Salute

19 ✦ Block 10: Star Flag

20 ✦ Block 11: Tail Fins

21 ✦ Block 12: String Star

22 ✦ Block 13: June Bug

23 ✦ Block 14: Peter Paul

24 ✦ Block 15: Bricks

25 ✦ Block 16: Origami

26 ✦ Block 17: For Connie

27 ✦ Block 18: Railroad

28 ✦ Block 19: Cross Corner

29 ✦ Block 20: Center Stage

30 ✦ Block 21: This-a-Way

31 ✦ Block 22: Star Shadow

32 ✦ Block 23: Clamshell

33 ✦ Block 24: Suspenders

34 ✦ Block 25: Ocean Waves

35 ✦ Block 26: Thorns

36 ✦ Block 27: Buckle

37 ✦ Block 28: Butterfly

38 ✦ Block 29: Happy Star

39 ✦ Block 30: Baby Bows

40 ✦ Block 31: Pendant

41 ✦ Block 32: Goslings

42 ✦ Block 33: Jigsaw

43 ✦ Block 34: Lattice

44 ✦ Block 35: Criss-Cross

45 ✦ Block 36: Lollipops

46 ✦ Block 37: Mrs. Nelson

47 ✦ Block 38: Big Wrench

48 ✦ Block 39: Nine-Patch Plaid

49 ✦ Block 40: Cathedral

50 ✦ Block 41: Sidewalk Chalk

51 ✦ Block 42: Twister

52 ✦ Block 43: Coverlet

53 ✦ Block 44: Tiller

54 ✦ Block 45: Star Struck

55 ✦ Block 46: Arrowhead

56 ✦ Block 47: Confused Geese

57 ✦ Block 48: January

58 ✦ Block 49: Double Take

59 ✦ Block 50: Patio

60 ✦ Block 51: Taffy

61 ✦ Block 52: Regatta

62 ✦ Block 53: Shoo Fly

63 ✦ Block 54: Vertically

64 ✦ Block 55: Knot

65 ✦ Block 56: Basket

66 ✦ Block 57: Wing Tips

67 ✦ Block 58: Intersection

68 ✦ Block 59: Facets

69 ✦ Block 60: Plaid

70 ✦ Block 61: Propeller

71 ✦ Block 62: Economy

72 ✦ Block 63: Game Board

73 ✦ Block 64: Tie Rack

74 ✦ Block 65: Anniversary

75 ✦ Block 66: Formal

76 ✦ Block 67: Savannah

77 ✦ Block 68: Stonegate

78 ✦ Block 69: Honeycomb

79 ✦ Block 70: Log Off

80 ✦ Block 71: Cousins

81 ✦ Block 72: Tomahawk

82 ✦ Block 73: Water Wheel

83 ✦ Block 74: Geese

84 ✦ Block 75: Confetti

85 ✦ Block 76: Zig Zag

86 ✦ Block 77: Hopscotch

87 ✦ Block 78: Split Wrench

88 ✦ Block 79: Lacewing

89 ✦ Block 80: Anvil

90 ✦ Block 81: Cherry-O

91 ✦ Block 82: Migration

92 ✦ Block 83: Four Rectangles

93 ✦ Block 84: Lanterns

94 ✦ Block 85: Red Cross

95 ✦ Block 86: Corners

96 ✦ Block 87: Good Night

97 ✦ Block 88: Album

98 ✦ Block 89: Spinning Spools

99 ✦ Block 90: Slant

100 ✦ Block 91: Hot Cross Buns

101 ✦ Block 92: Windows

102 ✦ Block 93: Formation

103 ✦ Block 94: Tuxedo

104 ✦ Block 95: Stellar

105 ✦ Block 96: Paw Prints

106 ✦ Block 97: Double Spot

107 ✦ Block 98: Upward

108 ✦ Block 99: Braid

109 ✦ Block 100: Double Dip

110 ✦ Block 101: Odd Ball

111 ✦ Block 102: Chevrons

112 ✦ Block 103: Bar Bells

113 ✦ Block 104: Wrong Way

114 ✦ Block 105: Whitestown

115 ✦ Block 106: House

116 ✦ Block 107: Stretch Dash

117 ✦ Block 108: Tree of Life

118 ✦ Block 109: Jailbird

119 ✦ Block 110: Time Pieces

120 ✦ Block 111: Turn Signal

121 ✦ Block 112: Wrench

122 ✦ Block 113: Rotini

123 ✦ Block 114: Skylights

124 ✦ Block 115: Simplicity

125 ✦ Block 116: Love Letter

126 ✦ Block 117: Apple Seeds

127 ✦ Block 118: Diagonal Stripes

128 ✦ Block 119: Checkers

129 ✦ Block 120: Tree

130 ✦ Block 121: Mainspring

131 ✦ Block 122: Fieldcrest

132 ✦ Block 123: Shooting Star

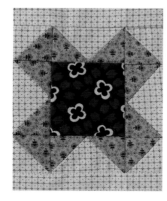

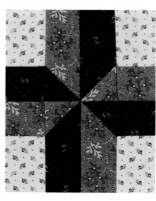
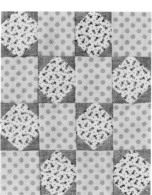

133 ✦ Block 124: Harlequin

134 ✦ Block 125: Good Luck

135 ✦ Block 126: John's Block

136 ✦ Block 127: Rook

137 ✦ Block 128: Skyscraper

138 ✦ Block 129: Cocktail

139 ✦ Block 130: Four Square

140 ✦ Block 131: Summer Time

141 ✦ Block 132: Monopoly

142 ✦ Block 133: Home Run

143 ✦ Block 134: Regiment

144 ✦ Block 135: Snowball Nines

145 ✦ Block 136: Comforter

146 ✦ Block 137: Pine Tree

147 ✦ Block 138: Gears

148 ✦ Block 139: Fields

149 ✦ Block 140: Ripples

150 ✦ Block 141: Sail Away

151 ✦ Block 142: Drum

152 ✦ Block 143: Patches

153 ✦ Block 144: Satchel

154 ✦ Block 145: Stairwell

155 ✦ Block 146: Pinwheel

156 ✦ Block 147: Big Spool

157 ✦ Block 148: Rodeo

158 ✦ Block 149: Bull's-Eye

159 ✦ Block 150: Woven

160 ✦ Block 151: The Extra Mile

161 ✦ Block 152: Cross Angle

162 ✦ Block 153: English Garden

163 ✦ Block 154: Lost Ship

164 ✦ Block 155: Snowball Fight

165 ✦ Block 156: Windmills

166 ✦ Block 157: Rafters

167 ✦ Block 158: Beehive

168 ✦ Block 159: Friendship Star

169 ✦ Block 160: Focus

170 ✦ Block 161: Apple Pie

171 ✦ Block 162: Courthouse Steps

172 ✦ Block 163: Flight

173 ✦ Block 164: Surrounded

174 ✦ Block 165: Zipper

175 ✦ Block 166: Dorothy

176 ✦ Block 167: Crazy

177 ✦ Block 168: Barrels

178 ✦ Block 169: Argyle

179 ✦ Block 170: Candy Cane

180 ✦ Block 171: Sapphire

181 ✦ Block 172: Fifteen Cents

182 ✦ Block 173: Split Star

183 ✦ Block 174: Framework

184 ✦ Block 175: Mountain View

185 ✦ Block 176: Blue Jay

186 ✦ Block 177: Aunt Nellie

187 ✦ Block 178: Crackers

188 ✦ Block 179: Steps

189 ✦ Block 180: Child's Play

190 ✦ Block 181: Old Maid

191 ✦ Block 182: Signature

192 ✦ Techniques

193 ✦ Patterns

202 ✦ Quilt Gallery

208 ✦ Acknowledgments

208 ✦ About the Authors

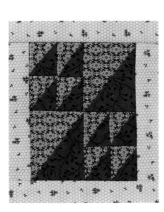

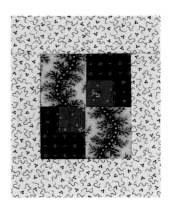

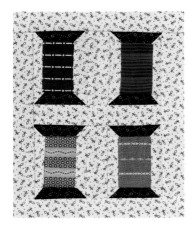

For many quilters, the friendships, connections, and camaraderie we develop as we share our passion for quilting with other women are as important as the quilts themselves. More than 25 years ago, we were part of a group of six women who began a special quilting relationship. Five were from the Lafayette, Indiana, area—Carol Hopkins, Pam Antalis, Garnet Roesel, and two others who, sadly, are no longer with us—and Linda Koenig lived in Whitestown, Indiana. With the common bond of similar fabric preferences and piecing skills, we exchanged scrappy half-square triangles for a year. We called these "Someday Squares," as in "Someday I'm going to make a quilt with these." Thus began a series of block exchanges in which we agreed on a particular block or type of block, the block size, a color palette, and the number of blocks to be made every month for a year. When the exchanges ended, each of us set the blocks in our own design, often finishing them just in time for a group display at a quilt show. Many of these quilts have been published in magazines, books, and individual patterns.

As we brainstormed ideas for our 2015 exchange, Linda proposed that we "design and assemble 4" × 5" quilt blocks using reproduction fabrics in blue, black, red, and double pink. Make four different blocks to share/keep each month for nine months." That sounded doable to the other three group members. But wait! Once we started, we found that there were no rectangular blocks to inspire us in books, magazines, computer software programs, or the numerous online offerings of sampler quilt blocks. Thus, we were charting a new path in block making that was both challenging and rewarding as we saw the pile of unique blocks grow. The blocks created by Garnet, Pam, Carol, and Linda as part of this group block exchange are showcased in their quilts pictured in the Quilt Gallery (page 202).

When Linda took her exchange blocks from the Lafayette group for show-and-tell with the North Stars, a group of 12 women with more diverse quilting interests that she meets with regularly, the enthusiasm for making 4" × 5" blocks was contagious. Right then and there, a challenge was in the making: "Create 4" × 5" blocks from either your own design or those from the Lafayette quilters using fabrics of your choice. Make as many blocks as you wish." The quilts that resulted from this challenge made by Theresa Arnold, Xenia Cord, Judy Barmann, Ruth Pedigo, and Mary Jane Teeters-Eichacker also appear in the Quilt Gallery.

Linda's quilt, The Sparrow's Window, pictured on page 202, is another story, for it combines the efforts of both groups and contains each and every block designed on behalf of the Lafayette group's exchange and the North Stars' challenge. With this book, we offer you the opportunity to select from these 182 unique blocks to create your own sampler quilt, large or small. While some blocks are modified versions of traditional blocks, many are brand-new, never-before-seen designs. We challenge you to make your own sampler blocks from your favorite colors and fabrics. When your quilting friends see what you're working on, we predict you just might find yourself participating in your own block exchange!

ONLINE QUILT GALLERY

Online you'll find full-color photos of quilts made from the blocks in this book. Visit ShopMartingale.com/anthology.html for gorgeous inspiration!

Sampler quilts emerged in the 19th century, offering an exciting alternative to the popular medallion or strippy settings that dominated the era. Many of the early sampler quilts, particularly the Baltimore Album quilts, were very formal looking, carefully planned and created from restricted color palettes and fabric styles. Other breathtaking antique scrap quilts, such as the iconic Jane Stickle quilt, contained a myriad of small prints in an assortment of colors that blended together well. Interestingly, watercolors and drawings of some early 1800s sampler quilts demonstrate that they were frequently made as group projects in which each person was assigned a block according to an overall plan.

With the resurgence of American quiltmaking in the 1970s, sampler quilts became the mainstay of beginning quilting classes. Typically, they were fashioned from just a few coordinating fabrics. A multicolored print was selected first, with four or five prints in complementary colors and contrast chosen next to complete the palette. Of course, you can take this same approach before making any of the blocks in this book. But perhaps you would have more fun making a sampler quilt from scraps!

Making a scrap quilt doesn't necessarily mean using just any leftover fabric that happens to be in your stash. You may wish to plan your quilt for particular colors and fabric styles, but regardless of what you choose, we encourage you to use lots of different fabrics. Once you have such a plan, you can go about gathering (or shopping for!) fabrics the whole time you're making the quilt. The plan for the blocks shown in this book called for reproduction-style prints in red, blue, black, and double pink. This may sound somewhat limited, but look at the photos below that show just some of the fabrics we used to see the resulting variety.

Notice that there are many different values of each of the four colors, resulting in light, medium, and dark pieces in each color family. If you've always thought that black needed to be used as a dark fabric, look what happens when a light black print gets paired with a dark blue fabric. Playing with fabrics is what gives you unlimited creativity when you're piecing quilt blocks and is what will truly create the personality of your quilt. We invite you to examine the quilts in our photo gallery to see the blocks in a variety of colors, fabric styles, and setting designs. Then it's time to start picking *your* fabrics.

*A small sample of the range of fabrics
used within the authors' color guidelines*

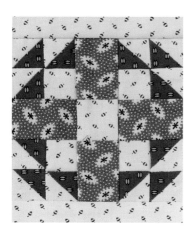

The patterns in this book provide the opportunity to make blocks you probably haven't made before, either because of their uncommon rectangular shape or because many were designed specifically for this project. There are many ways to use this book.

SAMPLER QUILTS

The Quilt Gallery on pages 202–207 includes sampler quilts made from different combinations and numbers of blocks found in this book. While the participants in the original block exchange used fabrics reminiscent of the late 1800s, the gallery quilts (both in this book and online; see "Online Quilt Gallery" on page 6) employ a variety of fabric styles. Select fabrics that showcase your color and style preferences, and enjoy the process of finding just the right blocks in which to use them.

SMALL QUILTS

Need a gift for a special friend? Have empty wall space that needs "a little something"? Just want to try a few new blocks that you haven't made before? Consider any of the following criteria when selecting a group of blocks for a small quilt:

+ Your favorite blocks
+ Easy blocks
+ Blocks with a theme, such as flying geese or stars
+ One block repeated in a variety of fabrics
+ Blocks of a certain color

CLUBS

We've all heard of book clubs. Why not organize a *block* club? A group leader—or, on a rotating basis, a club member—is responsible for selecting a block from the book, making it, and presenting it to the group along with any helpful construction hints. All group members (who need to have their own copy of the book) then make the block in their preferred fabrics and bring the completed blocks to the next meeting for an inspirational show-and-tell. Another option is to be more open-ended about block choices and encourage group members to make any block(s) they wish for the next meeting. Depending on how ambitious your group is, you may decide to make more than one block each month. After all, they're pretty small!

We suggest that the group pick a recurring day, time, and place to meet, such as 10:00 a.m. on the second Tuesday of each month at the Roasted Bean Coffee Shop. This way, no one has to clean house, bake, find enough chairs and good lighting, and do all the things we tell ourselves we have to do when quilters are coming over! Because there are no space or seating constraints, this arrangement easily accommodates guests or new members who are inspired by your blocks and want to join the group.

BLOCK EXCHANGES

We've participated in numerous quilt-block exchanges over the last 25 years, and we've learned invaluable, widely applicable lessons. Use the following suggestions as jumping-off points for organizing an exchange based on the blocks from this book.

+ **How do we get started?** Obviously, someone needs to get the ball rolling. Invite particular friends, or put out an open call for people who might be interested in trading blocks. Either way, this is the time to determine your maximum group size, since each member will be making blocks for everyone else in the group each month. We recommend limiting the group to four to six quilters who collect and sew with the same kind of fabrics you do, have the same expectations for accuracy, and perhaps most importantly, can consistently sew an accurate ¼" seam.

Once you've identified the participants, close the membership and stick with your decision. This can be hard to do, but it's necessary. From experience, we know that others will want to join your group once they see the wonderful blocks you're making. However, because none of us has unlimited quilting time, it's unfair to increase the number of blocks that the original group members agreed to make each month. Encourage latecomers to start a second group to mirror what your group is doing.

♦ **How many blocks does each group member make?** The group organizer can determine this in advance, or the participants can decide once the group has been established. In an exchange, each member makes sets of blocks using the agreed-upon color recipe or fabric style, and she makes the same set for each person in the group. For example, if your four-person group decides that you'll each make three different blocks a month, you'll need to make four of each of your three blocks for a total of 12 blocks. You'll give a set of three different blocks to each person in your group, and in return, you'll get three different blocks from each of them. Thus, you end up with 12 different blocks each month. Note that it's also important to establish in advance how many months the block exchange will last.

♦ **How do I know what blocks to make?** Determine which blocks each participant will make at the outset of the exchange. You can "count off" as we used to do in grade school, "1, 2, 3, 4, 1, 2, 3, 4," resulting in each member of a four-person group

making every fourth block in the book. Or, you may decide to divide the book into fourths, so that one person selects the blocks she makes from the first 45 blocks in the book, the second person selects hers from blocks 46 through 90, and so on. Other options include dividing the blocks by difficulty level, number of pieces, or construction technique, such as appliqué or paper piecing.

♦ **When and how do we exchange our blocks?** We've done this in two ways. One is to meet monthly at a restaurant, enjoy a meal together, and then exchange blocks. Everyone arrives excited to share the blocks they've made and to see what others have made for them. It's sort of like waiting for Santa to come!

The other option is to have everyone mail their blocks to the other participants any time before the month ends. This way, everyone can set a schedule that works best for them, and it's always a day-brightener to open the mailbox and find a squishy envelope inside. We found that we can send four of the blocks from this book in a business envelope with one first-class stamp.

♦ **What do we do with our blocks once the exchange ends?** The group should decide this at the start of the exchange. It may be that the group wants to exhibit all of the quilts together at a quilt show, in which case you'll need to set a deadline for finishing the quilts. Otherwise, we suggest that this decision be left to each participant. Either way, each person in the group will need to decide how to set her collection of blocks together. Let the fun begin!

Raspberries

WHAT YOU'LL NEED

- **A:** 6 light squares, 1⅞" × 1⅞"; cut the squares in half diagonally to yield 12 triangles
- **B:** 2 light rectangles, 1½" × 2"
- **C:** 2 red squares, 1⅞" × 1⅞"; cut the squares in half diagonally to yield 4 triangles
- **D:** 1 red square, 1½" × 1½"
- **E:** 1 pink #1 square, 2⅞" × 2⅞"; cut the square in half diagonally to yield 2 triangles
- **F:** 1 pink #2 square, 2⅞" × 2⅞"; cut the square in half diagonally to yield 2 triangles

ASSEMBLY

Press the seam allowances open after sewing each seam unless directed otherwise.

1. Referring to "Half-Square-Triangle Units" on page 192, sew four A triangles and the C triangles together in pairs to make four half-square-triangle units measuring 1½" square. Press the seam allowances toward the C triangles.

2. Sew A triangles to the right and bottom edges of each half-square-triangle unit. Make four (*fig. 1*).

3. Sew the E and F triangles to the units from step 2. Make two of each color, four total (*fig. 2*). Press the seam allowances toward the E and F triangles.

4. Lay out the step 3 units, the B rectangles, and the D square as shown. Sew the pieces together into three rows, and then join the rows (*fig. 3*).

Fig. 1

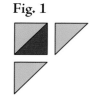

Make 4.

Fig. 2

Make 2 of each unit,
2½" × 2½".

Fig. 3

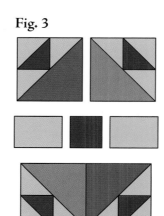

Chutes and Ladders

WHAT YOU'LL NEED

- **A:** 5 light squares, 1⅞" × 1⅞"; cut the squares in half diagonally to yield 10 triangles
- **B:** 2 light rectangles, 1" × 2½"
- **C:** 5 red check squares, 1⅞" × 1⅞"; cut the squares in half diagonally to yield 10 triangles
- **D:** 4 black check rectangles, 1" × 2½"
- **E:** 4 blue rectangles, 1" × 2½"

ASSEMBLY

Press the seam allowances open after sewing each seam unless directed otherwise.

1. Referring to "Half-Square-Triangle Units" on page 192, sew the A and C triangles together in pairs to make 10 half-square-triangle units measuring 1½" square. Press the seam allowances toward the C triangles.

2. Sew together the half-square-triangle units in two rows as shown, noting that the diagonal seams are mirror image in the second row (*fig. 1*).

3. Sew together the B, D, and E rectangles (*fig. 2*).

4. Sew the step 2 rows to opposite sides of the step 3 unit (*fig. 3*).

Fig. 1

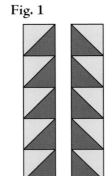

Make 1 of each unit,
1½" × 5½".

Fig. 2

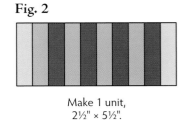

Make 1 unit,
2½" × 5½".

Fig. 3

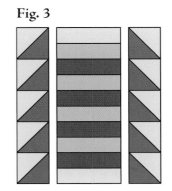

Oh-Oh!

WHAT YOU'LL NEED

- **A:** 4 light squares, 1¼" × 1¼"
- **B:** 4 light squares, 2" × 2"
- **C:** 2 blue rectangles, 1½" × 1¾"
- **D:** 4 blue rectangles, 2" × 2½"
- **E:** 2 blue rectangles, 1¼" × 1½"
- **F:** 4 black rectangles, 1¼" × 1½"
- **G:** 1 pink square, 1½" × 1½"

ASSEMBLY

Press the seam allowances open after sewing each seam unless directed otherwise.

1. Sew together a C rectangle and an F rectangle. Make two (*fig. 1*).

2. Draw a diagonal line from corner to corner on the wrong side of each A square and each B square. Referring to "Stitch-and-Flip Corners" on page 192, join a marked A square to the lower-right corner of a D rectangle. Join a marked B square to the upper-left corner of the D rectangle. Make two. Sew A and B squares to the lower-left and upper-right corners of a D rectangle, reversing the direction of the sewing line on the squares. Make two (*fig. 2*).

3. Arrange the units from steps 1 and 2, the E rectangles, the remaining F rectangles, and the G square as shown. Sew the pieces together into three rows, and then join the rows (*fig. 3*).

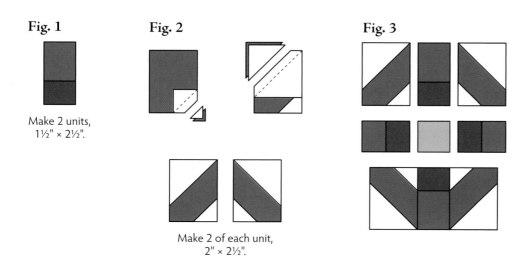

Fig. 1

Make 2 units,
1½" × 2½".

Fig. 2

Make 2 of each unit,
2" × 2½".

Fig. 3

Reflections

WHAT YOU'LL NEED

☐ **A:** 8 light squares, 1½" × 1½"
■ **B:** 8 assorted black rectangles, 1½" × 3"

ASSEMBLY

Press the seam allowances open after sewing each seam unless directed otherwise.

1. Draw a diagonal line from corner to corner on the wrong side of each A square.

2. Referring to "Stitch-and-Flip Corners" on page 192, join a marked A square to one end of a B rectangle. Make four (*fig. 1*).

3. Reversing the square placement and stitching direction as shown, repeat step 2 to make four reversed units (*fig. 2*).

4. Arrange the units from steps 2 and 3 as shown. Sew the units together into two rows, and then join the rows (*fig. 3*).

Fig. 1

Make 4 units,
1½" × 3".

Fig. 2

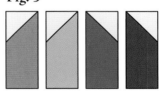

Make 4 units,
1½" × 3".

Fig. 3

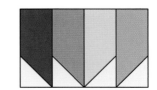

5 Quiver

WHAT YOU'LL NEED

- **A:** 2 red rectangles, 1" × 1½" (1 *each* of red #1 and red #3)
- **B:** 2 red rectangles, 1" × 2½" (1 *each* of red #2 and red #4)
- **C:** 4 red squares, 2¾" × 2¾" (1 *each* of red #1, #2, #3, and #4); cut the squares into quarters diagonally to yield 16 triangles (you'll have 8 left over)
- **D:** 2 light squares, 2⅜" × 2⅜"; cut the squares in half diagonally to yield 4 triangles
- **E:** 4 light rectangles, 1" × 1½"
- **F:** 4 light rectangles, 1" × 2½"
- **G:** 1 light rectangle, 1½" × 2½"

ASSEMBLY

Press the seam allowances open after sewing each seam unless directed otherwise.

1. Sew an E rectangle to each long side of the red #1 A rectangle. Make a second unit using the red #3 A rectangle (*fig. 1*).

2. Sew an F rectangle to each long side of the red #2 B rectangle. Make a second unit using the red #4 B rectangle (*fig. 2*).

3. Sew the C triangles together in pairs to make one *each* of the following combinations (*fig. 3*):
   - red #2 and red #1 • red #3 and red #2
   - red #1 and red #4 • red #4 and red #3

4. Sew a D triangle to each of the step 3 pairs. Make four (*fig. 4*). Press the seam allowances toward the darker triangles.

5. Arrange the units from steps 1, 2, and 4 and the G rectangle as shown. Sew the pieces together into three rows, and then join the rows (*fig. 5*).

Fig. 1

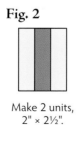

Make 2 units, 1½" × 2".

Fig. 2

Make 2 units, 2" × 2½".

Fig. 3

Make 1 of each unit.

Fig. 4

Make 4 units, 2" × 2".

Fig. 5

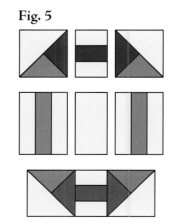

WHAT YOU'LL NEED

- **A:** 2 pink rectangles, 1½" × 2½"
- **B:** 2 pink rectangles, 1½" × 3½"
- **C:** 2 gray rectangles, 1½" × 2½"
- **D:** 4 gray squares, 1½" × 1½"
- **E:** 1 blue rectangle, 1½" × 2½"

ASSEMBLY

Press the seam allowances open after sewing each seam unless directed otherwise.

1. Sew together the A, C, and E rectangles (*fig. 1*).
2. Join a D square to each end of a B rectangle. Make two (*fig. 2*).
3. Sew the step 2 units to opposite sides of the step 1 unit (*fig. 3*).

Fig. 1

Make 1 unit, 2½" × 5½".

Fig. 2

Make 2 units, 1½" × 5½".

Fig. 3

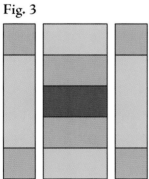

Thread

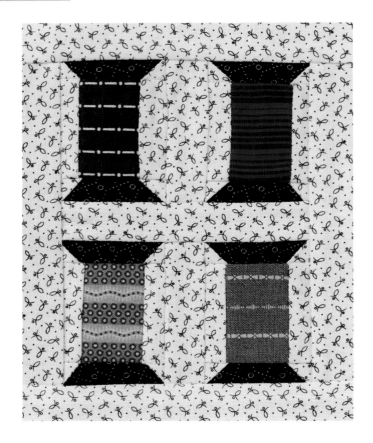

WHAT YOU'LL NEED

- **A:** 16 light squares, ¾" × ¾"
- **B:** 8 light rectangles, ¾" × 1¾"
- **C:** 2 light rectangles, 1" × 2¼"
- **D:** 1 light rectangle, 1" × 3½"
- **E:** 4 light rectangles, 1" × 4½"
- **F:** 8 black rectangles, ¾" × 1¾"
- **G:** 4 assorted stripe rectangles, 1¼" × 1¾"

ASSEMBLY

Press the seam allowances open after sewing each seam unless directed otherwise.

1. Draw a diagonal line from corner to corner on the wrong side of each A square. Referring to "Stitch-and-Flip Corners" on page 192, join a marked A square to each end of an F rectangle. Make eight (*fig. 1*).

2. Sew a B rectangle to each long side of a G rectangle. Sew step 1 units to the top and bottom of the unit. Make four (*fig. 2*).

3. Sew together two step 2 units and one C rectangle. Make two. Sew these units to the top and bottom of the D rectangle (*fig. 3*).

4. Sew E rectangles to opposite sides of the step 3 unit. Join the remaining E rectangles to the top and bottom of the unit (*fig. 4*).

Fig. 1

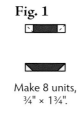

Make 8 units,
¾" × 1¾".

Fig. 2

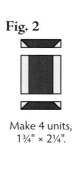

Make 4 units,
1¾" × 2¼".

Fig. 3

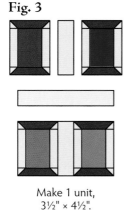

Make 1 unit,
3½" × 4½".

Fig. 4

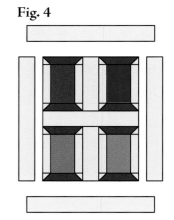

WHAT YOU'LL NEED

 A: 4 pink squares, 1½" × 1½"

B: 4 pink rectangles, 1" × 1¼"

C: 2 pink squares, 1" × 1"

D: 2 blue rectangles, 1½" × 2½"

E: 2 blue rectangles, 1¼" × 1½"

F: 1 blue rectangle, 1" × 1½"

G: 4 light rectangles, 1½" × 2¼"

H: 2 light rectangles, 1" × 1½"

I: 2 light rectangles, 1" × 4½"

ASSEMBLY

Press the seam allowances open after sewing each seam unless directed otherwise.

1. Draw a diagonal line from corner to corner on the wrong side of each A square. Referring to "Flying-Geese Units" on page 192, use the marked A squares and the D rectangles to make two flying-geese units.

2. Sew together two B rectangles and one E rectangle. Sew this unit to the bottom of a flying-geese unit. Make two (*fig. 1*).

3. Sew G rectangles to opposite sides of a step 2 unit. Make two (*fig. 2*).

4. Sew together the H rectangles, the C squares, and the F rectangle (*fig. 3*).

5. Arrange the units from steps 3 and 4 and the I rectangles as shown (*fig. 4*). Join the pieces.

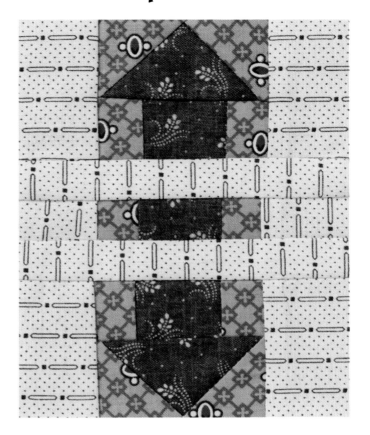

Fig. 1

Make 2 units,
2¼" × 2½".

Fig. 2

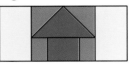

Make 2 units,
2¼" × 4½".

Fig. 3

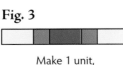

Make 1 unit,
1" × 4½".

Fig. 4

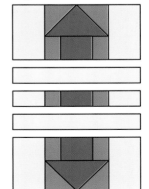

WHAT YOU'LL NEED

A: 4 blue squares, 1½" × 1½"

B: 2 blue rectangles, 1½" × 2½"

C: 4 black squares, 1½" × 1½"

D: 2 black rectangles, 1½" × 2½"

E: 2 black rectangles, 1" × 4½"

F: 4 light rectangles, 1" × 4½"

ASSEMBLY

Press the seam allowances open after sewing each seam unless directed otherwise.

1. Draw a diagonal line from corner to corner on the wrong side of each A square and each C square. Referring to "Flying-Geese Units" on page 192, use the marked A squares and the D rectangles to make two A/D flying-geese units. Using the marked C squares and the B rectangles, repeat to make two C/B flying-geese units (*fig. 1*).

2. Join the flying-geese units in a vertical row, alternating and rotating the A/D and C/B units as shown (*fig. 2*).

3. Sew one E rectangle and one F rectangle to each side of the step 2 unit as shown. Join the remaining F rectangles to the top and bottom of the unit (*fig. 3*).

Fig. 1

Make 2 of each unit, 1½" × 2½".

Fig. 2

Make 1 unit, 2½" × 4½".

Fig. 3

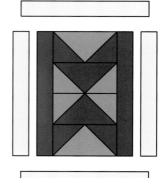

WHAT YOU'LL NEED

- ■ **A:** 16 blue squares, 1" × 1"
- ■ **B:** 2 blue squares, 1½" × 1½"
- □ **C:** 8 light rectangles, 1" × 1½"
- □ **D:** 8 light squares, 1" × 1"
- □ **E:** 4 light rectangles, 1" × 3½"
- ■ **F:** 4 red rectangles, 1" × 3½"

ASSEMBLY

Press the seam allowances open after sewing each seam unless directed otherwise.

1. Draw a diagonal line from corner to corner on the wrong side of each A square. Referring to "Flying-Geese Units" on page 192, use the marked A squares and the C rectangles to make eight flying-geese units.

2. Lay out four D squares, four flying-geese units, and a B square as shown. Sew the pieces together into three rows, and then join the rows. Make two (*fig. 1*).

3. Lay out the step 2 units and the F and E rectangles as shown. Sew the pieces together into two rows, and then join the rows (*fig. 2*).

Fig. 1

Make 2 units,
2½" × 2½".

Fig. 2

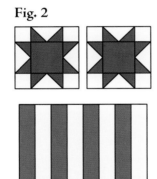

Tail Fins

WHAT YOU'LL NEED

■ **A:** 16 blue squares, 1½" × 1½"
□ **B:** 8 assorted pink rectangles, 1½" × 3"

ASSEMBLY

Press the seam allowances open after sewing each seam unless directed otherwise.

1. Draw a diagonal line from corner to corner on the wrong side of each A square.

2. Referring to "Stitch-and-Flip Corners" on page 192, join a marked A square to each end of a B rectangle. Make four (*fig. 1*).

3. Reversing the stitching directions as shown, repeat step 2 to make four reversed units (*fig. 1*).

4. Arrange the units from steps 2 and 3 as shown. Sew the units together into two rows, and then join the rows (*fig. 2*).

Fig. 1

Fig. 2

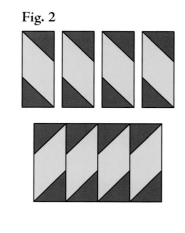

Make 4 of each unit,
1½" × 3".

WHAT YOU'LL NEED

■ **Positions 1–4, 7–10, 13–16, and 19–22:**
16 assorted blue, pink, and red scraps, about 2½" × 2½"

■ **Positions 5, 6, 11, 12, 17, 18, 23, and 24:**
8 light scraps, about 2¼" × 3¾"

1 photocopy or tracing *each* of String Star paper-foundation piecing patterns A–D (page 193)

ASSEMBLY

1. Using the prepared patterns and the assorted blue, pink, red, and light scraps, paper piece the four sections of the block. Refer to the photo and the illustrated, downloadable Paper-Foundation Piecing tutorial at ShopMartingale.com/HowtoQuilt as needed.

2. Join the step 1 sections into two rows, and then sew the rows together (*fig. 1*). Press the seam allowances open. Press the block with a medium-hot iron, and then remove the foundation papers.

Fig. 1

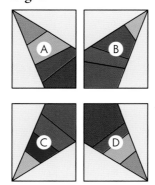

June Bug

WHAT YOU'LL NEED

☐ **A:** 4 light squares, 1⅞" × 1⅞"; cut the squares in half diagonally to yield 8 triangles

☐ **B:** 6 light squares, 1½" × 1½"

▨ **C:** 4 blue squares, 1⅞" × 1⅞"; cut the squares in half diagonally to yield 8 triangles

▨ **D:** 2 blue rectangles, 1½" × 2½"

■ **E:** 1 navy rectangle, 2½" × 3½"

ASSEMBLY

Press the seam allowances open after sewing each seam unless directed otherwise.

1. Referring to "Half-Square-Triangle Units" on page 192, sew the A and C triangles together in pairs to make eight half-square-triangle units measuring 1½" square. Press the seam allowances toward the C triangles.

2. Sew together four half-square-triangle units and one B square. Make two (*fig. 1*).

3. Draw a diagonal line from corner to corner on the wrong side of the remaining B squares. Referring to "Flying-Geese Units" on page 192, use the marked B squares and the D rectangles to make two flying-geese units.

4. Sew the flying-geese units to the top and bottom of the E rectangle. Join the step 2 units to opposite sides of the unit (*fig. 2*).

Fig. 1 **Fig. 2**

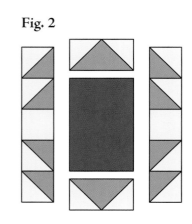

Make 2 units,
1½" × 5½".

WHAT YOU'LL NEED

☐ **A and B:** 1 pink rectangle, 7" × 9"

■ **C:** 1 red rectangle, 4½" × 5½"

ASSEMBLY

1. Using the patterns below, and referring to the appliqué template instructions on page 192, cut two A pieces and two B pieces from the pink 7" × 9" rectangle. Prepare the curved edges of the pieces for your preferred appliqué method.

2. Referring to the photo for guidance, position the A pieces at the top and bottom of the C rectangle, and position the B pieces on the sides of the C rectangle. Pin or baste them in place.

3. Use your preferred appliqué method to sew each piece to the C rectangle. Carefully press the block with a pressing cloth, or turn the block over and press on the wrong side.

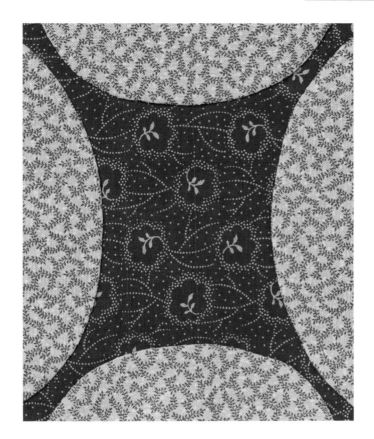

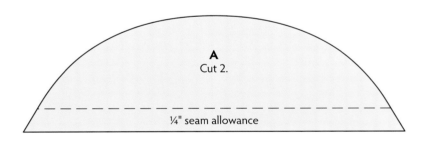

A
Cut 2.

¼" seam allowance

Patterns include seam allowances
on straight edges only. For hand
appliqué, add seam allowances
along the curved edges.

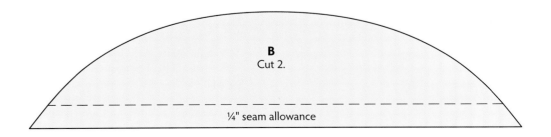

B
Cut 2.

¼" seam allowance

Bricks

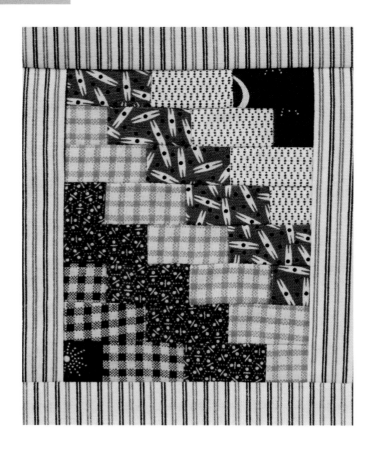

WHAT YOU'LL NEED

■ **Medium blue:** 1 square, 1" x 1"; 5 rectangles, 1" × 1½"

□ **Light:** 1 square, 1" x 1"; 3 rectangles, 1" × 1½"

■ **Navy:** 2 squares, 1" x 1"; 1 rectangle, 1" × 1½"

▨ **Pink check:** 2 squares, 1" x 1"; 5 rectangles, 1" × 1½"

■ **Black:** 1 square, 1" x 1"; 4 rectangles, 1" × 1½"

▨ **Black check:** 1 square, 1" x 1"; 2 rectangles, 1" × 1½"

▨ **Black stripe:** 4 rectangles, 1" × 4½"

ASSEMBLY

Press the seam allowances open after sewing each seam unless directed otherwise.

1. Lay out the squares and rectangles as shown. Sew the pieces together into eight rows. Trim the seam allowances to ⅛". Join the rows; trim as before (*fig. 1*).

2. Sew black stripe rectangles to opposite sides of the step 1 unit. Join the remaining black stripe rectangles to the top and bottom of the unit (*fig. 2*).

Fig. 1

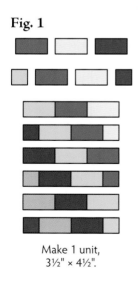

Make 1 unit,
3½" × 4½".

Fig. 2

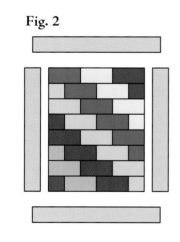

WHAT YOU'LL NEED

 **A:** 4 assorted dark rectangles, 1½" × 3½"

 **B:** 16 light squares, 1" × 1"

 **C:** 4 light rectangles, 1" × 4½"

ASSEMBLY

Press the seam allowances open after sewing each seam unless directed otherwise.

1. Draw a diagonal line from corner to corner on the wrong side of each B square. Referring to "Stitch-and-Flip Corners" on page 192, join a marked B square to each corner of an A rectangle. Make four (*fig. 1*).

2. Join the step 1 units as shown (*fig. 2*).

3. Sew C rectangles to opposite sides of the step 2 unit. Join the remaining C rectangles to the top and bottom of the unit (*fig. 3*).

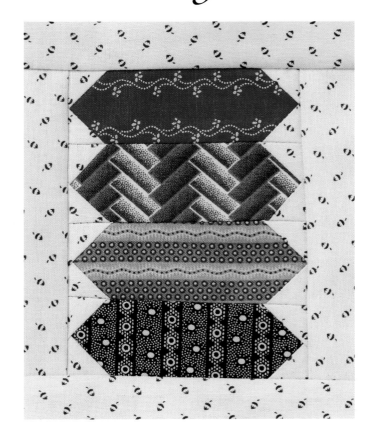

Fig. 1

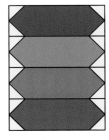

Make 4 units,
1½" × 3½".

Fig. 2

Make 1 unit,
3½" × 4½".

Fig. 3

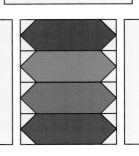

For Connie

WHAT YOU'LL NEED

☐ **A:** 1 light strip, 1" × 14"
■ **B:** 1 black strip, 1" × 14"
■ **C:** 4 black squares, 1½" × 1½"
■ **D:** 1 red rectangle, 2½" × 3½"

ASSEMBLY

Press the seam allowances open after sewing each seam unless directed otherwise.

1. Join the A and B strips along the long edges to make a strip set. From the strip set, cut two segments measuring 1½" × 2½" and two segments measuring 1½" × 3½" (*fig. 1*).

2. Arrange the segments from step 1, the C squares, and the D rectangle as shown. Join the pieces into three rows, and then join the rows (*fig. 2*).

Fig. 1

2½"   3½"

1½"

Cut 2 of each segment.

Fig. 2

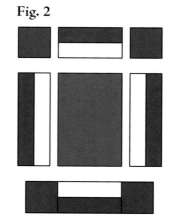

WHAT YOU'LL NEED

A: 15 blue rectangles, 1" × 1½"

B: 15 light rectangles, 1" × 1½"

C: 2 black rectangles, 1" × 5½"

ASSEMBLY

Press the seam allowances open after sewing each seam unless directed otherwise.

1. Sew together five A rectangles and five B rectangles. Make three (*fig. 1*).

2. Arrange the step 1 units and the C rectangles in five rows. Sew the rows together (*fig. 2*).

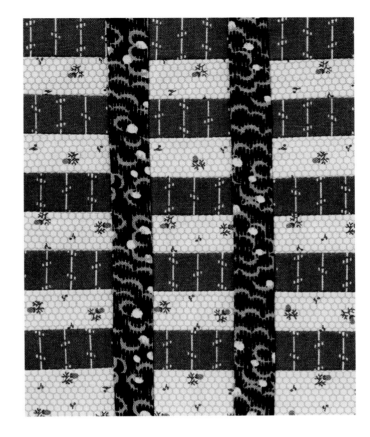

Fig. 1

Make 3 units,
1½" × 5½".

Fig. 2

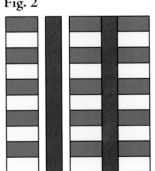

19 *Cross Corner*

WHAT YOU'LL NEED

■ **A:** 4 red squares, 1¼" × 1¼"
■ **B:** 1 red square, 1½" × 1½"
■ **C:** 4 pink rectangles, 2" × 2½"
□ **D:** 2 gray rectangles, 1½" × 2½"
□ **E:** 2 gray rectangles, 1½" × 2"

ASSEMBLY

Press the seam allowances open after sewing each seam unless directed otherwise.

1. Draw a diagonal line from corner to corner on the wrong side of each A square.
2. Referring to "Stitch-and-Flip Corners" on page 192, join a marked A square to the lower-right corner of a C rectangle. Make two (*fig. 1*).
3. Reversing the square placement and stitching direction as shown, repeat step 2 to make two reversed units (*fig. 2*).
4. Arrange the units from steps 2 and 3, the D and E rectangles, and the B square (*fig. 3*). Sew the pieces together into three rows, and then join the rows.

Fig. 1

Make 2 units,
2" × 2½".

Fig. 2

Make 2 units,
2" × 2½".

Fig. 3

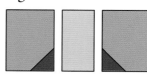

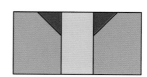

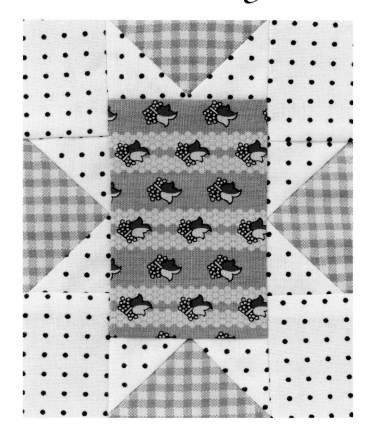

WHAT YOU'LL NEED

☐ **A:** 8 light squares, 1½" × 1½"

☐ **B:** 4 light rectangles, 1½" × 2"

▢ **C:** 4 blue check rectangles, 1½" × 2½"

▢ **D:** 1 blue stripe rectangle, 2½" × 3½"

ASSEMBLY

Press the seam allowances open after sewing each seam unless directed otherwise.

1. Draw a diagonal line from corner to corner on the wrong side of each A square. Referring to "Flying-Geese Units" on page 192, use the marked A squares and the C rectangles to make four flying-geese units.

2. Sew a B rectangle to each end of a flying-geese unit. Make two (*fig. 1*).

3. Sew flying-geese units to the top and bottom of the D rectangle (*fig. 2*).

4. Join the step 2 units to opposite sides of the step 3 unit (*fig. 3*).

Fig. 1

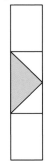

Make 2 units,
1½" × 5½".

Fig. 2

Make 1 unit,
2½" × 5½".

Fig. 3

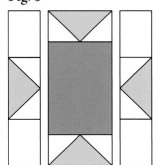

This-a-Way

WHAT YOU'LL NEED

Positions 1–10: 20 assorted red and black scraps, about 1½" × 4"

☐ **A:** 4 light rectangles, 1" × 4½"

2 photocopies or tracings of the This-a-Way paper-foundation piecing pattern (page 194)

ASSEMBLY

1. Using the prepared patterns and the assorted red and black scraps, paper piece the two sections of the block. Refer to the photo and the illustrated, downloadable Paper-Foundation Piecing tutorial at ShopMartingale.com/HowtoQuilt as needed.

2. Join the step 1 sections to make the block center (*fig. 1*); press the seam allowances open. Press the block center with a medium-hot iron, and then remove the foundation papers.

3. Sew A rectangles to opposite sides of the block center. Join the remaining A rectangles to the top and bottom of the unit (*fig. 2*). Press the seam allowances open.

Fig. 1

Make 1 unit,
3½" × 4½".

Fig. 2

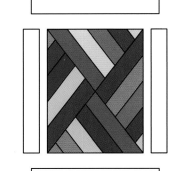

Star Shadow

WHAT YOU'LL NEED

 A: 8 light squares, 1½" × 1½"

B: 2 light squares, 1⅞" × 1⅞"; cut the squares in half diagonally to yield 4 triangles

C: 4 blue rectangles, 1½" × 2½"

D: 2 black squares, 1⅞" × 1⅞"; cut the squares in half diagonally to yield 4 triangles

E: 2 black rectangles, 1" × 4½"

ASSEMBLY

Press the seam allowances open after sewing each seam unless directed otherwise.

1. Draw a diagonal line from corner to corner on the wrong side of four A squares. Referring to "Stitch-and-Flip Corners" on page 192, join a marked A square to one end of a C rectangle. Make four (*fig. 1*).

2. Referring to "Half-Square-Triangle Units" on page 192, sew the B and D triangles together in pairs to make four half-square-triangle units measuring 1½" square. Press the seam allowances toward the D triangles.

3. Sew an A square to the top of a half-square-triangle unit to make a vertical row. Join a step 1 unit to the right side of the row. Make four (*fig. 2*).

4. Join the step 3 units in pairs, rotating them as shown, and then sew the pairs together. Sew the E rectangles to the top and bottom of the unit (*fig. 3*).

Fig. 1

Make 4 units, 1½" × 2½".

Fig. 2

Make 4 units, 2½" × 2½".

Fig. 3

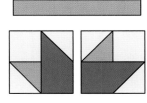

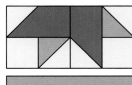

Clamshell

WHAT YOU'LL NEED

A: 13 assorted black, red, blue, and pink squares, 3" × 3"

B: 1 light rectangle, 3½" × 4½"

C: 4 light rectangles, 1" × 4½"

ASSEMBLY

Press the seam allowances open after sewing each seam unless directed otherwise.

1. Using the pattern on page 194, cut 13 clamshell pieces from the A squares. Turn under the top curve of each clamshell piece a scant ¼" and baste it in place (*fig. 1*).

2. Layer two prepared clamshell pieces with right sides together. Find the place where the top curve meets the side of the clamshell, and take three small whipstitches on top of each other to join them. Repeat to form a row of three clamshells (*fig. 2*). Make three rows of three clamshells and two rows of two clamshells.

3. Starting ¼" from the top of the B rectangle, use small whipstitches to appliqué a row of three clamshells to the rectangle. Referring to the photo for guidance, appliqué alternating rows of two and three clamshells for a total of five rows; position each new clamshell row so that it hides the joining stitches of the previous row. Carefully press the unit with a pressing cloth, or turn the unit over and press on the wrong side.

4. Trim the sides and bottom of the step 3 unit so that it measures 3½" × 4½". Sew C rectangles to opposite sides of the unit. Join the remaining C rectangles to the top and bottom of the unit (*fig. 3*). Remove the basting stitches from the clamshells.

Fig. 1
Baste.
Make 13.

Fig. 2
Stitch.   Stitch.

Fig. 3

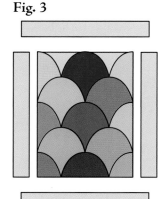

WHAT YOU'LL NEED

A: 2 light stripe squares, 2½" × 2½"

B: 4 light stripe rectangles, 1½" × 2"

C: 8 navy squares, 1½" × 1½"

D: 2 navy rectangles, 2" × 2½"

ASSEMBLY

Press the seam allowances open after sewing each seam unless directed otherwise.

1. Draw a diagonal line from corner to corner on the wrong side of each C square. Referring to "Stitch-and-Flip Corners" on page 192, join a marked C square to each corner of an A square. Make two (*fig. 1*).

2. Arrange the step 1 units and the B and D rectangles as shown. Sew the pieces together into three rows, and then join the rows (*fig. 2*).

Fig. 1

Make 2 units,
2½" × 2½".

Fig. 2

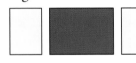

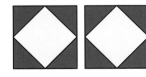

Ocean Waves

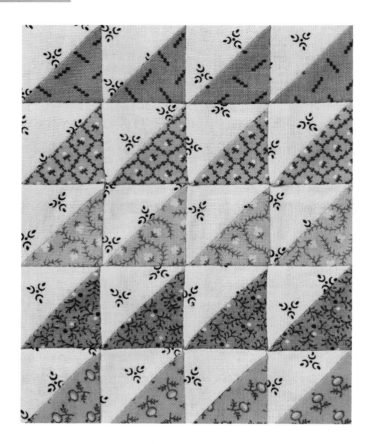

WHAT YOU'LL NEED

☐ **A:** 10 light squares, 1⅞" × 1⅞"; cut the squares in half diagonally to yield 20 triangles

☐ **B:** 10 assorted pink squares, 1⅞" × 1⅞" (2 *each* of 5 different prints); cut the squares in half diagonally to yield 20 triangles

ASSEMBLY

Press the seam allowances open after sewing each seam unless directed otherwise.

1. Referring to "Half-Square-Triangle Units" on page 192, sew the A and B triangles together in pairs to make 20 half-square-triangle units measuring 1½" square (*fig. 1*). Press the seam allowances toward the B triangles.

2. Lay out the half-square-triangle units as shown, placing matching units in each horizontal row. Join the units into five rows, and then sew the rows together (*fig. 2*).

Fig. 1

Make 20 units,
1½" × 1½".

Fig. 2

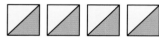
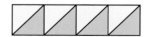
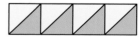
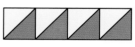

WHAT YOU'LL NEED

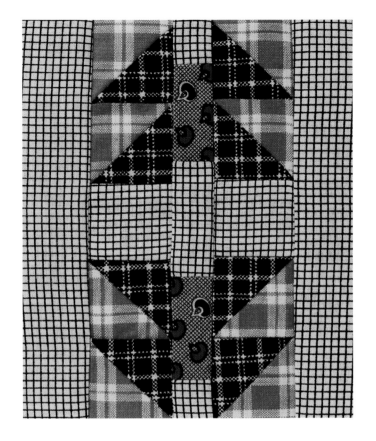

- **A:** 4 pink plaid squares, 1⅞" × 1⅞"; cut the squares in half diagonally to yield 8 triangles
- **B:** 4 black plaid squares, 1⅞" × 1⅞"; cut the squares in half diagonally to yield 8 triangles
- **C:** 2 light check squares, 1½" × 1½"
- **D:** 2 light check squares, 1" × 1"
- **E:** 1 light check rectangle, 1" × 2"
- **F:** 2 light check rectangles, 1¼" × 5½"
- **G:** 2 blue rectangles, 1" × 1¾"

ASSEMBLY

Press the seam allowances open after sewing each seam unless directed otherwise.

1. Referring to "Half-Square-Triangle Units" on page 192, sew the A and B triangles together in pairs to make eight half-square-triangle units measuring 1½" square. Press the seam allowances toward the B triangles.

2. Sew together four half-square-triangle units and a C square. Make two (*fig. 1*).

3. Sew together the D squares and the G and E rectangles (*fig. 2*).

4. Arrange the units from steps 2 and 3 and the F rectangles in five rows as shown. Sew the rows together (*fig. 3*).

Fig. 1

Make 2 units,
1½" × 5½".

Fig. 2

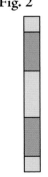

Make 1 unit,
1" × 5½".

Fig. 3

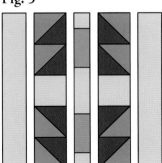

Buckle

WHAT YOU'LL NEED

- **A:** 4 blue check rectangles, 1¼" × 1½"
- **B:** 2 blue check rectangles, 1" × 1½"
- **C:** 4 blue check squares, 1½" × 1½"
- **D:** 2 black rectangles, 1" × 1½"
- **E:** 1 black square, 1½" × 1½"
- **F:** 2 blue rectangles, 1½" × 3½"
- **G:** 2 blue rectangles, 1½" × 2½"

ASSEMBLY

Press the seam allowances open after sewing each seam unless directed otherwise.

1. Lay out the A, D, and B rectangles and the E square as shown. Sew the pieces together into three rows, and then join the rows (*fig. 1*).
2. Arrange the step 1 unit, the C squares, and the G and F rectangles as shown. Sew the pieces together into three rows, and then join the rows (*fig. 2*).

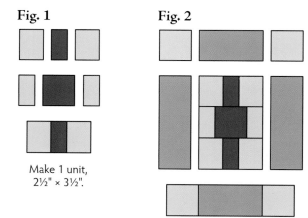

Fig. 1

Make 1 unit,
2½" × 3½".

Fig. 2

WHAT YOU'LL NEED

 A: 2 light rectangles, 1½" × 2"

B: 2 red rectangles, 1½" × 2"

C: 2 red rectangles, 1½" × 2½"

D: 2 blue squares, 2½" × 2½"

E: 2 pink rectangles, 2½" × 3"

ASSEMBLY

Press the seam allowances open after sewing each seam unless directed otherwise.

1. Sew together an A rectangle and a B rectangle to make a pair. Join a C rectangle to the top of the pair. Make two (*fig. 1*).

2. Draw a diagonal line from corner to corner on the wrong side of each D square. Referring to "Stitch-and-Flip Corners" on page 192, join a marked D square to one end of an E rectangle. Make two (*fig. 2*).

3. Arrange the units from steps 1 and 2 as shown. Sew the units together into two rows, and then join the rows (*fig. 3*).

Fig. 1

Make 2 units, 2½" × 3".

Fig. 2

Make 2 units, 2½" × 3".

Fig. 3

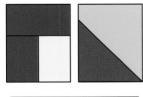

Happy Star

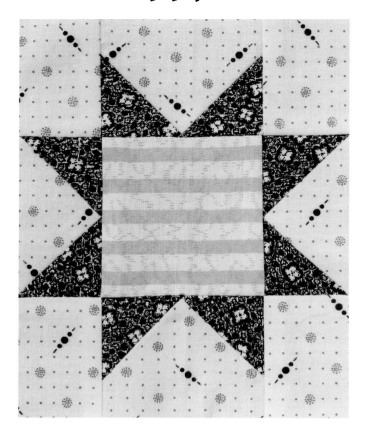

WHAT YOU'LL NEED

☐ **A:** 2 light rectangles, 2" × 2½"

☐ **B:** 2 light rectangles, 1½" × 2½"

☐ **C:** 4 light rectangles, 1½" × 2"

■ **D:** 8 black squares, 1½" × 1½"

☐ **E:** 1 pink stripe square, 2½" × 2½"

ASSEMBLY

Press the seam allowances open after sewing each seam unless directed otherwise.

1. Draw a diagonal line from corner to corner on the wrong side of each D square.

2. Referring to "Stitch-and-Flip Corners" on page 192, join marked D squares to both the lower-left and lower-right corners of an A rectangle. Make two (*fig. 1*).

3. Join a marked D square to each end of a B rectangle as in step 2. Make two (*fig. 2*).

4. Arrange the units from steps 2 and 3, the C rectangles, and the E square as shown. Sew the pieces together into three rows, and then join the rows (*fig. 3*).

Fig. 1

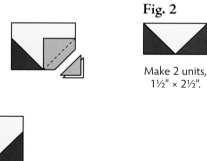

Make 2 units,
2" × 2½".

Fig. 2

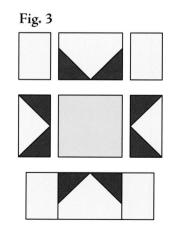

Make 2 units,
1½" × 2½".

Fig. 3

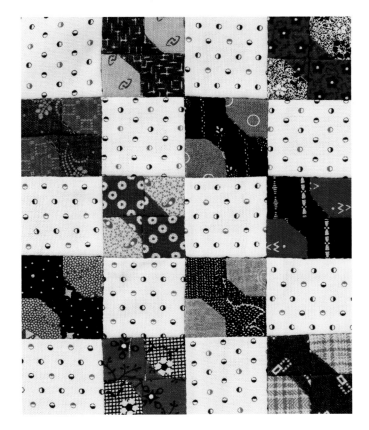

WHAT YOU'LL NEED

- **A:** 10 light squares, 1½" × 1½"
- **B:** 20 assorted dark squares, 1" × 1"
  (2 *each* of 10 different prints)
- **C:** 20 assorted dark squares, ¾" × ¾"
  (2 *each* of the 10 prints used for B squares)
- **D:** 20 assorted medium squares, 1" × 1"
  (2 *each* of 10 different prints)

ASSEMBLY

Press the seam allowances open after sewing each seam unless directed otherwise.

1. Draw a diagonal line from corner to corner on the wrong side of each C square. Referring to "Stitch-and-Flip Corners" on page 192, join a marked C square to one corner of a D square. Repeat to make a second unit with the same fabrics. Make 10 pairs of two matching units each, 20 units total (*fig. 1*).

2. Arrange a pair of matching step 1 units and two matching B squares as shown. Sew the pieces together into two rows, and then join the rows. Make 10 (*fig. 2*).

3. Lay out the step 2 units and the A squares as shown. Sew the pieces together into five rows, and then join the rows (*fig. 3*).

Fig. 1

Make 20 units, 1" × 1"
(10 pairs of 2 matching units).

Fig. 2

Make 10 units,
1½" × 1½".

Fig. 3

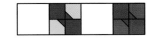

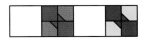

Pendant

WHAT YOU'LL NEED

- **A:** 8 gray squares, 1" × 1"
- **B:** 8 gray squares, 1¼" × 1¼"
- **C:** 4 gray rectangles, 1½" × 2"
- **D:** 2 gray rectangles, 1" × 3½"
- **E:** 2 navy squares, 1½" × 1½"
- **F:** 1 navy square, 2" × 2"
- **G:** 2 navy rectangles, 1¼" × 2"
- **H:** 2 navy rectangles, 1¼" × 3½"

ASSEMBLY

Press the seam allowances open after sewing each seam unless directed otherwise.

1. Draw a diagonal line from corner to corner on the wrong side of each A square. Referring to "Stitch-and-Flip Corners" on page 192, join a marked A square to each corner of an E square. Make two (*fig. 1*).

2. Draw a diagonal line from corner to corner on the wrong side of each B square. Join a marked B square to each corner of the F square as in step 1. Sew the G rectangles to the sides of the unit (*fig. 2*).

3. Join a marked B square to each end of an H rectangle as in step 1. Make two (*fig. 3*).

4. Sew the step 3 units to the top and bottom of the step 2 unit (*fig. 4*).

5. Arrange the units from steps 1 and 4 and the C and D rectangles as shown. Sew the pieces together into three rows, and then join the rows (*fig. 5*).

Fig. 1

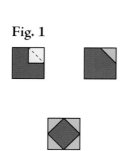

Make 2 units,
1½" × 1½".

Fig. 2

Make 1 unit,
2" × 3½".

Fig. 3

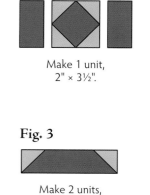

Make 2 units,
1¼" × 3½".

Fig. 4

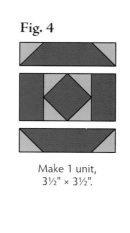

Make 1 unit,
3½" × 3½".

Fig. 5

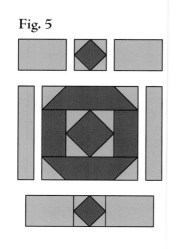

WHAT YOU'LL NEED

A: 10 light squares, 1½" × 1½"

B: 5 assorted red, black, and blue rectangles, 1½" × 2½"

C: 2 pink rectangles, 1½" × 5½"

ASSEMBLY

Press the seam allowances open after sewing each seam unless directed otherwise.

1. Draw a diagonal line from corner to corner on the wrong side of each A square. Referring to "Flying-Geese Units" on page 192, use the marked A squares and the B rectangles to make five flying-geese units.

2. Join the flying-geese units in a vertical row (*fig. 1*).

3. Sew the C rectangles to opposite sides of the step 2 row (*fig. 2*).

Fig. 1

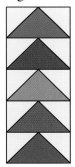

Make 1 unit, 2½" × 5½".

Fig. 2

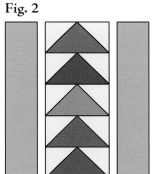

WHAT YOU'LL NEED

- **A:** 7 light squares, 1⅞" × 1⅞"; cut the squares in half diagonally to yield 14 triangles
- **B:** 7 blue squares, 1⅞" × 1⅞"; cut the squares in half diagonally to yield 14 triangles
- **C:** 1 red rectangle, 2½" × 3½"

ASSEMBLY

Press the seam allowances open after sewing each seam unless directed otherwise.

1. Referring to "Half-Square-Triangle Units" on page 192, sew the A and B triangles together in pairs to make 14 half-square-triangle units measuring 1½" square. Press the seam allowances toward the B triangles.

2. Sew together three half-square-triangle units. Make two (*fig. 1*).

3. Sew together four half-square-triangle units, rotating the unit at the left end 90° as shown. Make two (*fig. 2*).

4. Sew the step 2 units to opposite sides of the C rectangle, noting the color placement. Join the step 3 units to the top and bottom of the unit, again noting the color placement (*fig. 3*).

Fig. 1

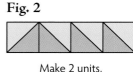

Make 2 units,
1½" × 3½".

Fig. 2

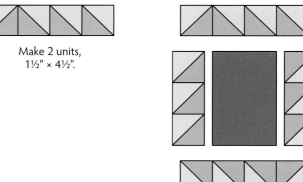

Make 2 units,
1½" × 4½".

Fig. 3

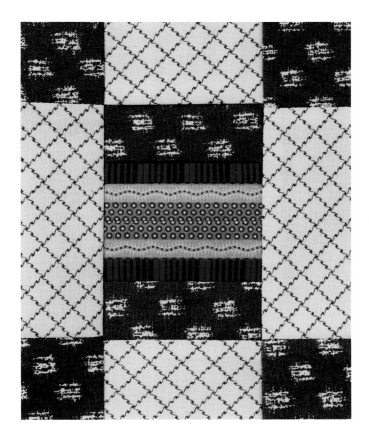

WHAT YOU'LL NEED

- **A:** 2 blue rectangles, 1¼" × 2½"
- **B:** 4 blue squares, 1½" × 1½"
- **C:** 2 red rectangles, ¾" × 2½"
- **D:** 2 pink stripe rectangles, 1" × 2½"
- **E:** 2 light rectangles, 1½" × 3½"
- **F:** 2 light rectangles, 1½" × 2½"

ASSEMBLY

Press the seam allowances open after sewing each seam unless directed otherwise.

1. Sew together the A, C, and D rectangles (*fig. 1*). Trim the seam allowances to ⅛".

2. Arrange the step 1 unit, the B squares, and the F and E rectangles as shown. Sew the pieces together into three rows, and then join the rows (*fig. 2*).

Fig. 1

Fig. 2

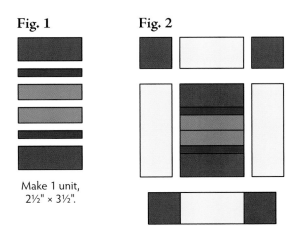

Make 1 unit, 2½" × 3½".

Criss-Cross

WHAT YOU'LL NEED

- **A:** 4 light rectangles, 1⅝" × 2⅛"
- **B:** 4 pink rectangles, 1" × 2⅛"
- **C:** 4 pink rectangles, 1" × 1⅝"
- **D:** 4 pink rectangles, 1" × 1¼"
- **E:** 2 black rectangles, 1¼" × 2⅛"
- **F:** 4 black squares, 1" × 1"
- **G:** 2 black rectangles, 1¼" × 1⅝"
- **H:** 1 black square, 1¼" × 1¼"

ASSEMBLY

Press the seam allowances open after sewing each seam unless directed otherwise.

1. Sew together two A rectangles, two B rectangles, and one E rectangle. Make two (*fig. 1*).
2. Sew together two C rectangles, two F squares, and one D rectangle. Make two (*fig. 2*).
3. Sew together the G rectangles, two D rectangles, and the H square (*fig. 3*).
4. Arrange the units from steps 1–3 as shown (*fig. 4*). Join the units.

Fig. 1

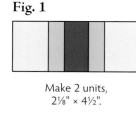

Make 2 units,
2⅛" × 4½".

Fig. 2

Make 2 units,
1" × 4½".

Fig. 3

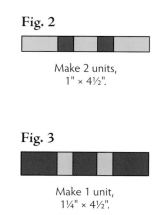

Make 1 unit,
1¼" × 4½".

Fig. 4

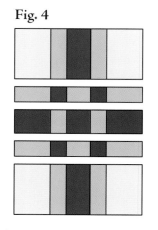

WHAT YOU'LL NEED

 A: 16 light squares, 1⅛" × 1⅛"

B: 4 assorted red and blue rectangles, 2½" × 3"

ASSEMBLY

Press the seam allowances open after sewing each seam unless directed otherwise.

1. Draw a diagonal line from corner to corner on the wrong side of each A square. Referring to "Stitch-and-Flip Corners" on page 192, join a marked A square to each corner of a B rectangle. Make four (*fig. 1*).

2. Arrange the units from step 1 as shown. Sew the units together into two rows, and then join the rows (*fig. 2*).

Fig. 1

Make 4 units,
2½" × 3".

Fig. 2

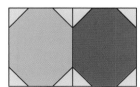

Mrs. Nelson

WHAT YOU'LL NEED

- **A:** 4 red squares, 1⅝" × 1⅝"; cut the squares in half diagonally to yield 8 triangles
- **B:** 4 red squares, 1¼" × 1¼"
- **C:** 1 red square, 1" × 1"
- **D:** 4 light squares, 1⅝" × 1⅝"; cut the squares in half diagonally to yield 8 triangles
- **E:** 4 light squares, 1¼" × 1¼"
- **F:** 4 light rectangles, 1¼" × 2"
- **G:** 4 light rectangles, ¾" × 2¾"
- **H:** 2 blue rectangles, 1" × 2¼"
- **I:** 2 blue rectangles, 1" × 2¾"

ASSEMBLY

Press the seam allowances open after sewing each seam unless directed otherwise.

1. Referring to "Half-Square-Triangle Units" on page 192, sew the A and D triangles together in pairs to make eight half-square-triangle units measuring 1¼" square. Press the seam allowances toward the A triangles.

2. Arrange two half-square-triangle units, a B square, and an E square as shown. Sew the pieces together into two rows, and then join the rows. Make four (*fig. 1*).

3. Orienting the units as shown, sew an F rectangle to each step 2 unit. Make two of each (*fig. 2*).

4. Arrange the step 3 units; the G, H, and I rectangles; and the C square as shown. Sew the pieces together into three rows, and then join the rows (*fig. 3*).

Fig. 1

Make 4 units,
2" × 2".

Fig. 2

Make 2 of each unit,
2" × 2¾".

Fig. 3

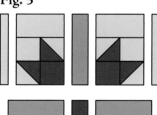

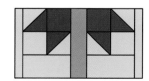

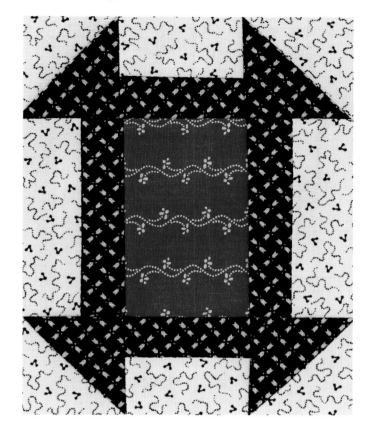

WHAT YOU'LL NEED

- **A:** 2 light squares, 2⅛" × 2⅛"; cut the squares in half diagonally to yield 4 triangles
- **B:** 2 light rectangles, 1¼" × 2"
- **C:** 2 light rectangles, 1¼" × 3"
- **D:** 2 black squares, 2⅛" × 2⅛"; cut the squares in half diagonally to yield 4 triangles
- **E:** 2 black rectangles, 1" × 2"
- **F:** 2 black rectangles, 1" × 3"
- **G:** 1 red rectangle, 2" × 3"

ASSEMBLY

Press the seam allowances open after sewing each seam unless directed otherwise.

1. Referring to "Half-Square-Triangle Units" on page 192, sew the A and D triangles together in pairs to make four half-square-triangle units measuring 1¾" square. Press the seam allowances toward the D triangles.

2. Sew together a B rectangle and an E rectangle. Make two (*fig. 1*).

3. Sew together a C rectangle and an F rectangle. Make two (*fig. 2*).

4. Arrange the units from steps 1–3 and the G rectangle as shown. Sew the pieces together into three rows, and then join the rows (*fig. 3*).

Fig. 1

Make 2 units, 1¾" × 2".

Fig. 2

Make 2 units, 1¾" × 3".

Fig. 3

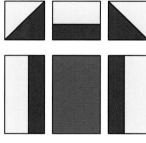

Nine-Patch Plaid

WHAT YOU'LL NEED

A: 24 assorted blue squares, 1" × 1"
B: 21 light squares, 1" × 1"
C: 2 light rectangles, 1½" × 2"
D: 2 light rectangles, 1" × 2"
E: 2 black check rectangles, ¾" × 5"
F: 2 black check rectangles, ¾" × 4½"

ASSEMBLY

Press the seam allowances open after sewing each seam unless directed otherwise.

1. Arrange five A squares and four B squares as shown. Sew the pieces together into three rows, and then join the rows. Trim the seam allowances to ⅛". Make four (*fig. 1*).

2. Arrange four A squares and five B squares as shown. Sew the pieces together into three rows, and then join the rows (*fig. 2*). Trim as in step 1.

3. Lay out the units from steps 1 and 2 and the D and C rectangles as shown. Sew the pieces together into three rows, and then join the rows (*fig. 3*).

4. Sew the E rectangles to opposite sides of the step 3 unit. Join the F rectangles to the top and bottom of the unit (*fig. 4*).

Fig. 1

Make 4 units,
2" × 2".

Fig. 2

Make 1 unit,
2" × 2".

Fig. 3

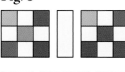

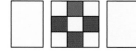

Make 1 unit,
4" × 5".

Fig. 4

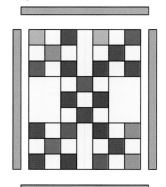

WHAT YOU'LL NEED

A: 1 red square, 7" × 7"

B: 1 tan plaid rectangle, 3½" × 4½"

C: 4 light rectangles, 1" × 4½"

ASSEMBLY

Press the seam allowances open after sewing each seam unless directed otherwise.

1. Using the pattern below, and referring to the appliqué template instructions on page 192, cut two A pieces and two A reversed pieces from the red 7" square. Prepare the curved edges of the pieces for your preferred appliqué method.

2. Referring to the photo for guidance, position the A and A reversed pieces on the four corners of the B rectangle. Pin or baste them in place.

3. Use your preferred appliqué method to sew each piece to the B rectangle. Carefully press the appliquéd rectangle with a pressing cloth, or turn it over and press on the wrong side.

4. Sew C rectangles to opposite sides of the step 3 unit. Join the remaining C rectangles to the top and bottom of the unit (*fig. 1*).

Fig. 1

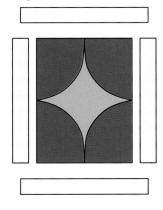

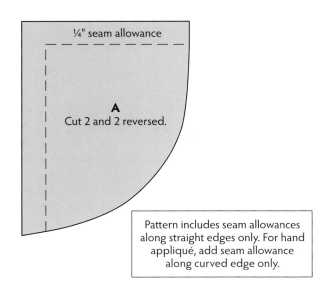

¼" seam allowance

A
Cut 2 and 2 reversed.

Pattern includes seam allowances along straight edges only. For hand appliqué, add seam allowance along curved edge only.

Sidewalk Chalk

WHAT YOU'LL NEED

- **A:** 6 light rectangles, 1" × 1½"
- **B:** 4 light squares, 1½" × 1½"
- **C:** 3 assorted pink rectangles, 1½" × 2"
- **D:** 3 assorted blue rectangles, 1½" × 2"
- **E:** 2 blue stripe rectangles, 1½" × 2½"

ASSEMBLY

Press the seam allowances open after sewing each seam unless directed otherwise.

1. Sew together two A rectangles, one C rectangle, and one D rectangle. Make three (*fig. 1*).
2. Sew together two B squares and one E rectangle. Make two (*fig. 2*).
3. Arrange the units from steps 1 and 2 as shown (*fig. 3*). Join the units.

Fig. 1

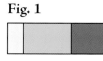

Make 3 units,
1½" × 4½".

Fig. 2

Make 2 units,
1½" × 4½".

Fig. 3

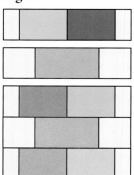

WHAT YOU'LL NEED

A: 4 pink squares, 1½" × 1½"

B: 2 light rectangles, 1½" × 3"

C: 2 light rectangles, 1¾" × 2½"

D: 2 blue rectangles, 1½" × 3"

E: 2 blue rectangles, 1¾" × 2½"

ASSEMBLY

Press the seam allowances open after sewing each seam unless directed otherwise.

1. Draw a diagonal line from corner to corner on the wrong side of each A square.

2. Referring to "Stitch-and-Flip Corners" on page 192, join a marked A square to one end of a B rectangle. Make two (*fig. 1*).

3. Join a marked A square to the lower-left corner of a C rectangle as in step 2. Make two (*fig. 2*).

4. Sew each step 2 unit to a D rectangle, and sew each step 3 unit to an E rectangle. Make two of each (*fig. 3*).

5. Arrange the units from step 4 as shown. Sew the units together into two rows, and then join the rows (*fig. 4*).

Fig. 1

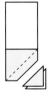

Make 2 units,
1½" × 3".

Fig. 2

Make 2 units,
1¾" × 2½".

Fig. 3

Make 2 of each unit,
2½" × 3".

Fig. 4

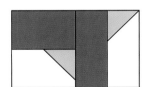

Coverlet

WHAT YOU'LL NEED

A: 20 assorted medium and dark squares, 1½" × 1½"

ASSEMBLY

Press the seam allowances open after sewing each seam unless directed otherwise.

1. Sew together four A squares in a row. Make five (*fig. 1*).
2. Join the step 1 units as shown (*fig. 2*).

Fig. 1

Make 5 units,
1½" × 4½".

Fig. 2

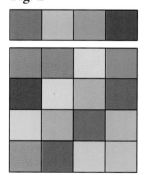

WHAT YOU'LL NEED

A: 8 blue squares, 1⅜" × 1⅜"; cut the squares in half diagonally to yield 16 triangles

B: 8 light squares, 1⅜" × 1⅜"; cut the squares in half diagonally to yield 16 triangles

C: 4 light squares, 1" × 1"

D: 4 light rectangles, 1" × 2"

E: 2 light rectangles, 1¼" × 4"

F: 2 light rectangles, 1¼" × 4½"

G: 1 black rectangle, 1" × 2"

ASSEMBLY

Press the seam allowances open after sewing each seam unless directed otherwise.

1. Referring to "Half-Square-Triangle Units" on page 192, sew the A and B triangles together in pairs to make 16 half-square-triangle units measuring 1" square. Press the seam allowances toward the A triangles. Trim the seam allowances to ⅛".

2. Sew together four half-square-triangle units and a C square. Trim as in step 1. Make four (*fig. 1*).

3. Sew D rectangles to opposite sides of the G rectangle. Join the remaining D rectangles to the top and bottom of the unit (*fig. 2*).

4. Sew step 2 units to opposite sides of the step 3 unit. Join the remaining step 2 units to the top and bottom of the unit (*fig. 3*).

5. Sew the E rectangles to opposite sides of the step 4 unit. Join the F rectangles to the top and bottom of the unit (*fig. 4*).

Fig. 1

Make 4 units,
1" × 3".

Fig. 2

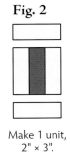

Make 1 unit,
2" × 3".

Fig. 3

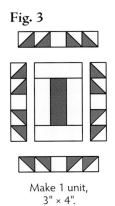

Make 1 unit,
3" × 4".

Fig. 4

Star Struck

WHAT YOU'LL NEED

- **A:** 7 red squares, 1" × 1"
- **B:** 1 red square, 1½" × 1½"
- **C:** 7 black #1 squares, 1" × 1"
- **D:** 1 black #1 square, 1½" × 1½"
- **E:** 2 black #2 rectangles, 1" × 3½"
- **F:** 2 black #2 rectangles, 1" × 5½"
- **G:** 6 light rectangles, 1" × 1½"
- **H:** 2 light squares, 1" × 1"
- **I:** 2 light squares, 1½" × 1½"
- **J:** 2 light rectangles, 1" × 2"
- **K:** 2 light rectangles, 1" × 3½"

ASSEMBLY

Press the seam allowances open after sewing each seam unless directed otherwise.

1. Draw a diagonal line from corner to corner on the wrong side of each A square and each C square. Referring to "Flying-Geese Units" on page 192, use four marked A squares and two G rectangles to make two red flying-geese units. Using four marked C squares and two G rectangles, make two black flying-geese units (*fig. 1*).

2. Arrange an H square, the red flying-geese units, and the B square as shown. Sew the pieces together into two rows, and then join the rows. Repeat, using the remaining H square, the black flying-geese units, and the D square. Make one of each (*fig. 2*).

3. Referring to "Stitch-and-Flip Corners" on page 192, join one marked A square and two marked C squares to three corners of an I square. Reversing the triangle colors in the corners, repeat using two A squares and one C square. Make one of each (*fig. 3*).

4. Join a G rectangle to each step 3 unit as shown, and then sew a J rectangle to an adjacent side. Make one of each (*fig. 4*).

5. Arrange the units from steps 2 and 4 as shown. Sew the units together into two rows, and then join the rows (*fig. 5*).

6. Sew each E rectangle to a K rectangle to make two rectangle pairs. Sew the rectangle pairs to the top and bottom of the step 5 unit as shown. Sew the F rectangles to opposite sides of the unit (*fig. 6*).

Fig. 1

Make 2 of each unit,
1" × 1½".

Fig. 2

Make 1 of each unit,
2" × 2".

Fig. 3

Make 1 of each unit,
1½" × 1½".

Fig. 4

Make 1 of each unit,
2" × 2".

Fig. 5

Make 1 unit,
3½" × 3½".

Fig. 6

WHAT YOU'LL NEED

A: 6 light squares, 1⅝" × 1⅝"; cut the squares in half diagonally to yield 12 triangles

B: 4 light rectangles, 1½" × 2¾"

C: 1 light square, 1" × 1"

D: 6 blue squares, 1⅝" × 1⅝"; cut the squares in half diagonally to yield 12 triangles

E: 2 red rectangles, 1" × 2¾"

F: 2 red rectangles, 1" × 2¼"

ASSEMBLY

Press the seam allowances open after sewing each seam unless directed otherwise.

1. Referring to "Half-Square-Triangle Units" on page 192, sew the A and D triangles together in pairs to make 12 half-square-triangle units measuring 1¼" square. Press the seam allowances toward the D triangles.

2. Sew the half-square-triangle units together in groups of three as shown. Make two of each unit, noting the change in seam directions (*fig. 1*).

3. Sew a B rectangle to each step 2 unit as shown, noting the change in rectangle placement. Make two of each (*fig. 2*).

4. Arrange the step 3 units, the E and F rectangles, and the C square (*fig. 3*). Sew the pieces together into three rows, and then join the rows.

Fig. 1

Make 2 of each unit, 1¼" × 2¾".

Fig. 2

Make 2 of each unit, 2¼" × 2¾".

Fig. 3

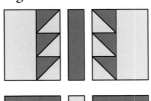

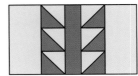

Confused Geese

WHAT YOU'LL NEED

- **A:** 16 light squares, 1½" × 1½"
- **B:** 4 light rectangles, 1" × 2½"
- **C:** 2 black rectangles, 1½" × 2½"
- **D:** 2 pink rectangles, 1½" × 2½"
- **E:** 2 red rectangles, 1½" × 2½"
- **F:** 2 blue rectangles, 1½" × 2½"

ASSEMBLY

Press the seam allowances open after sewing each seam unless directed otherwise.

1. Draw a diagonal line from corner to corner on the wrong side of each A square. Referring to "Flying-Geese Units" on page 192, use the marked A squares and the C, D, E, and F rectangles to make eight flying-geese units (four pairs of two matching units).

2. Join two matching flying-geese units and a B rectangle in a row. Make two (*fig. 1*).

3. Sew together two matching flying-geese units to make a pair, noting the change in the direction of the geese. Join a B rectangle to the top of the pair. Make two (*fig. 2*).

4. Arrange the units from steps 2 and 3 as shown. Sew the units together into two rows, and then join the rows (*fig. 3*).

Fig. 1

Make 2 units,
2½" × 3".

Fig. 2

Make 2 units,
2½" × 3".

Fig. 3

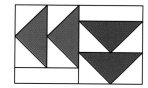

WHAT YOU'LL NEED

 A: 1 blue rectangle, 2" × 2½"

B: 2 pink rectangles, 1" × 2½"

C: 2 black rectangles, 1¼" × 3"

D: 2 light rectangles, 1¼" × 4"

E: 2 light rectangles, 1¼" × 4½"

ASSEMBLY

Press the seam allowances open after sewing each seam unless directed otherwise.

1. Sew the B rectangles to opposite sides of the A rectangle (*fig. 1*).

2. Sew the C rectangles to the top and bottom of the step 1 unit (*fig. 2*).

3. Sew the D rectangles to opposite sides of the step 2 unit. Join the E rectangles to the top and bottom of the unit (*fig. 3*).

Fig. 1

Make 1 unit,
2½" × 3".

Fig. 2

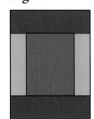

Make 1 unit,
3" × 4".

Fig. 3

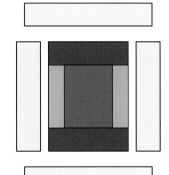

Double Take

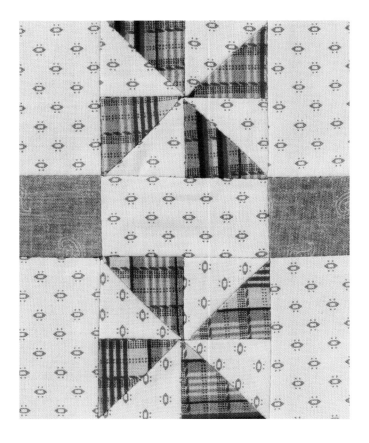

WHAT YOU'LL NEED

☐ **A:** 4 light squares, 1⅞" × 1⅞"; cut the squares in half diagonally to yield 8 triangles

☐ **B:** 5 light rectangles, 1½" × 2½"

■ **C:** 4 plaid squares, 1⅞" × 1⅞"; cut the squares in half diagonally to yield 8 triangles

■ **D:** 2 blue squares, 1½" × 1½"

ASSEMBLY

Press the seam allowances open after sewing each seam unless directed otherwise.

1. Referring to "Half-Square-Triangle Units" on page 192, sew the A and C triangles together in pairs to make eight half-square-triangle units measuring 1½" square. Press the seam allowances toward the C triangles.

2. Sew together four half-square-triangle units in pairs, and then join the pairs. Make two (*fig. 1*).

3. Arrange the step 2 units, the B rectangles, and the D squares as shown. Sew the pieces together into three rows, and then join the rows (*fig. 2*).

Fig. 1

Make 2 units,
2½" × 2½".

Fig. 2

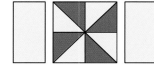

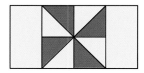

WHAT YOU'LL NEED

 **A:** 4 pink #1 squares, 1½" × 1½"

B: 1 pink #2 rectangle, 2½" × 3½"

C: 2 light rectangles, 1½" × 2½"

D: 2 light rectangles, 1½" × 3½"

ASSEMBLY

Press the seam allowances open after sewing each seam unless directed otherwise.

1. Sew an A square to each end of a C rectangle. Make two (*fig. 1*).

2. Sew the D rectangles to opposite sides of the B rectangle (*fig. 2*).

3. Arrange the units from steps 1 and 2 (*fig. 3*). Join the units.

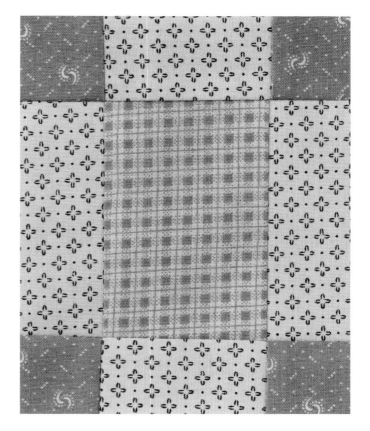

Fig. 1

Make 2 units,
1½" × 4½".

Fig. 2

Make 1 unit,
3½" × 4½".

Fig. 3

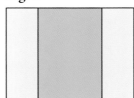

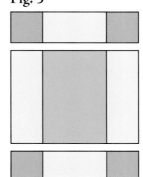

Taffy

WHAT YOU'LL NEED

☐ **A:** 36 light squares, 1" × 1"

☐ **B:** 2 light rectangles, 1" × 5½"

■ ■ **C:** 6 dark squares, 1½" × 1½"
(2 *each* of black #1, black #2, and red)

■ ■ **D:** 3 dark rectangles, 1½" × 3½"
(1 *each* of black #1, black #2, and red)

ASSEMBLY

Press the seam allowances open after sewing each seam unless directed otherwise.

1. Draw a diagonal line from corner to corner on the wrong side of each A square.

2. Referring to "Stitch-and-Flip Corners" on page 192, join a marked A square to each corner of a C square. Make three sets of two matching units, six units total (*fig. 1*).

3. Join a marked A square to each corner of a D rectangle as in step 2. Make three (*fig. 2*).

4. Using matching units, sew together two step 2 units and a step 3 unit. Make three (*fig. 3*).

5. Arrange the step 4 units and the B rectangles as shown (*fig. 4*). Join the pieces.

Fig. 1

Make 6 units, 1½" × 1½"
(3 sets of 2 matching units).

Fig. 2

Make 3 units,
1½" × 3½".

Fig. 3

Make 3 units,
1½" × 5½".

Fig. 4

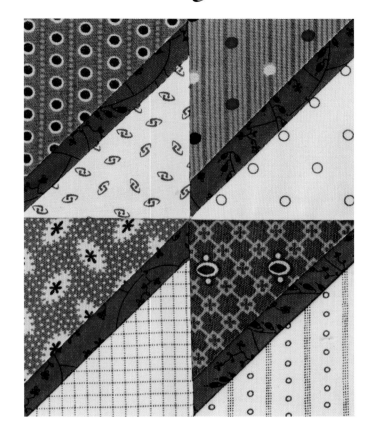

WHAT YOU'LL NEED

■ **A:** 4 red rectangles, 2½" × 3"

■ **B:** 4 assorted blue squares, 2½" × 2½"

□ **C:** 4 assorted light squares, 2½" × 2½"

ASSEMBLY

Press the seam allowances open after sewing each seam unless directed otherwise.

1. Draw a diagonal line from corner to corner on the wrong side of each B square and each C square. Referring to "Stitch-and-Flip Corners" on page 192, join a marked B square to one end of an A rectangle. Join a marked C square to the opposite end of the A rectangle. Make four (*fig. 1*).

2. Arrange the step 1 units as shown. Sew the units together into two rows, and then join the rows (*fig. 2*).

Fig. 1

Fig. 2

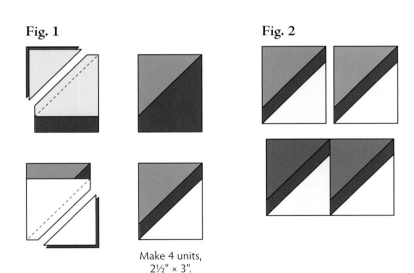

Make 4 units, 2½" × 3".

Shoo Fly

WHAT YOU'LL NEED

☐ **A:** 2 light squares, 1⅞" × 1⅞"; cut the squares in half diagonally to yield 4 triangles

☐ **B:** 2 light rectangles, 1½" × 2½"

☐ **C:** 2 light rectangles, 1½" × 3½"

■ **D:** 2 red squares, 1⅞" × 1⅞"; cut the squares in half diagonally to yield 4 triangles

■ **E:** 1 red plaid rectangle, 2½" × 3½"

ASSEMBLY

Press the seam allowances open after sewing each seam unless directed otherwise.

1. Referring to "Half-Square-Triangle Units" on page 192, sew the A and D triangles together in pairs to make four half-square-triangle units measuring 1½" square. Press the seam allowances toward the D triangles.

2. Sew a half-square-triangle unit to each end of a B rectangle. Make two (*fig. 1*).

3. Sew the C rectangles to opposite sides of the E rectangle (*fig. 2*).

4. Arrange the units from steps 2 and 3 as shown (*fig. 3*). Join the units.

Fig. 1

Make 2 units,
1½" × 4½".

Fig. 2

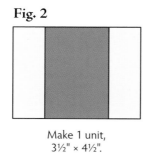

Make 1 unit,
3½" × 4½".

Fig. 3

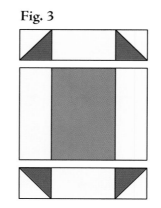

WHAT YOU'LL NEED

A: 8 assorted pink, blue, and black rectangles, 1" × 2"

B: 4 assorted pink, blue, and black rectangles, 1" × 2½"

☐ **C:** 2 light rectangles, 1½" × 5½"

ASSEMBLY

Press the seam allowances open after sewing each seam unless directed otherwise.

1. Sew together four A rectangles side by side. Make two (*fig. 1*).

2. Sew together the B rectangles side by side (*fig. 2*).

3. Arrange the units from steps 1 and 2 in a vertical row as shown. Join the units. Sew the C rectangles to opposite sides of the row (*fig. 3*).

Fig. 1

Make 2 units,
2" × 2½".

Fig. 2

Make 1 unit,
2½" × 2½".

Fig. 3

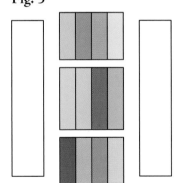

Knot

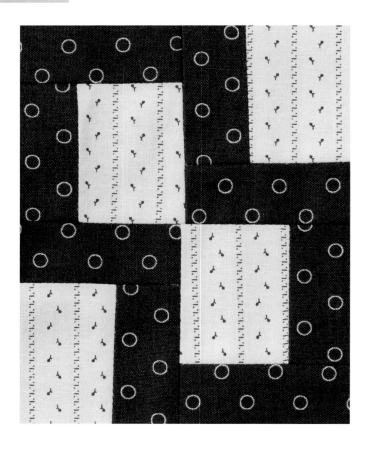

WHAT YOU'LL NEED

A: 4 light rectangles, 1¾" × 2¼"
B: 4 navy rectangles, 1¼" × 2¼"
C: 4 navy rectangles, 1¼" × 2½"

ASSEMBLY

Press the seam allowances open after sewing each seam unless directed otherwise.

1. Sew together an A rectangle and a B rectangle. Make four (*fig. 1*).

2. Sew a C rectangle to the top of a step 1 unit; make two. Join a C rectangle to the bottom of a step 1 unit; make two (*fig. 2*).

3. Arrange the step 2 units as shown. Sew the units together into two rows, and then join the rows (*fig. 3*).

Fig. 1

Make 4 units,
2¼" × 2½".

Fig. 2

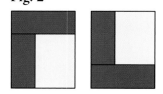

Make 2 of each unit,
2½" × 3".

Fig. 3

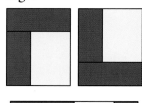

WHAT YOU'LL NEED

- **A–C:** 1 red square, 7" × 7"
- **D:** 1 red check square, 4" × 4"
- **E:** 1 red check rectangle, 2½" × 3½"
- **F:** 4 light rectangles, 1" × 4½"

ASSEMBLY

Press the seam allowances open after sewing each seam unless directed otherwise.

1. Using the patterns on page 194, and referring to the patchwork and appliqué template instructions on page 192, cut one A triangle, two B triangles, and one C handle from the red 7" square, and cut two D triangles from the red check 4" square.

2. Sew together a B triangle and a D triangle as shown. Repeat to make a second unit, noting the reversed position of the triangles (*fig. 1*).

3. Join the step 2 units to the A triangle (*fig. 2*).

4. Prepare the curved edges of the C handle for your preferred appliqué method, and appliqué it to the E rectangle. Sew this unit to the top of the step 3 unit (*fig. 3*).

5. Sew F rectangles to opposite sides of the step 4 unit. Join the remaining F rectangles to the top and bottom of the unit (*fig. 4*).

Fig. 1

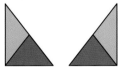

Make 1 of each unit.

Fig. 2

Make 1 unit, 2½" × 3½".

Fig. 3

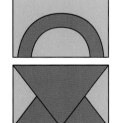

Make 1 unit, 3½" × 4½".

Fig. 4

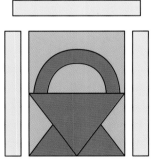

Wing Tips

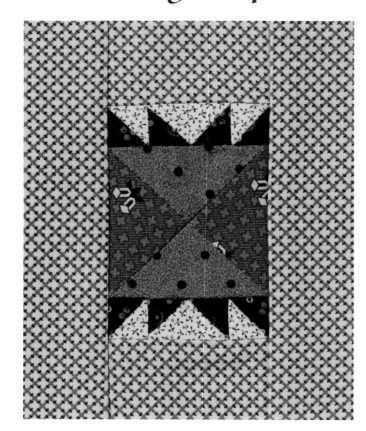

WHAT YOU'LL NEED

☐ **A:** 4 light squares, 1⅜" × 1⅜"; cut the squares in half diagonally to yield 8 triangles

■ **B:** 4 navy squares, 1⅜" × 1⅜"; cut the squares in half diagonally to yield 8 triangles

■ **C:** 1 blue square, 3¼" × 3¼"; cut the square into quarters diagonally to yield 4 triangles (you'll have 2 left over)

■ **D:** 1 red square, 3¼" × 3¼"; cut the square into quarters diagonally to yield 4 triangles (you'll have 2 left over)

☐ **E:** 2 gray rectangles, 1½" × 2½"

☐ **F:** 2 gray rectangles, 1½" × 5½"

ASSEMBLY

Press the seam allowances open after sewing each seam unless directed otherwise.

1. Referring to "Half-Square-Triangle Units" on page 192, sew the A and B triangles together in pairs to make eight half-square-triangle units measuring 1" square. Trim the seam allowances to ⅛", and press them toward the B triangles.

2. Sew together four half-square-triangle units, noting the seam directions. Trim as in step 1. Make two (*fig. 1*).

3. Sew together a C triangle and a D triangle. Make two (*fig. 2*). Join the pairs to make a quarter-square-triangle unit measuring 2½" square.

4. Arrange the step 2 units, the quarter-square-triangle unit, and the E rectangles in a vertical row as shown. Join the pieces. Sew the F rectangles to opposite sides of the row (*fig. 3*).

Fig. 1

Make 2 units,
1" × 2½".

Fig. 2

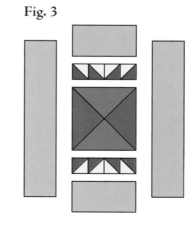

Make 1 unit,
2½" × 2½".

Fig. 3

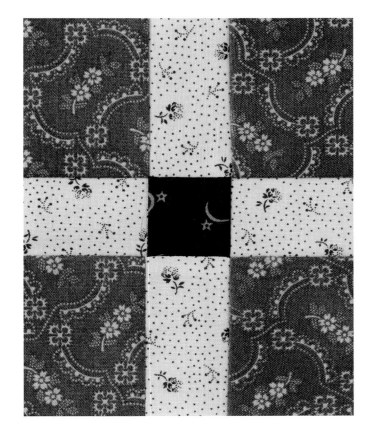

WHAT YOU'LL NEED

A: 4 blue rectangles, 2" × 2½"

B: 2 light rectangles, 1½" × 2½"

C: 2 light rectangles, 1½" × 2"

D: 1 black square, 1½" × 1½"

ASSEMBLY

Press the seam allowances open after sewing each seam unless directed otherwise.

1. Sew A rectangles to opposite sides of a B rectangle. Make two (*fig. 1*).

2. Sew the C rectangles to opposite sides of the D square (*fig. 2*).

3. Arrange the units from steps 1 and 2 as shown (*fig. 3*). Join the units.

Fig. 1

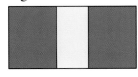

Make 2 units,
2½" × 4½".

Fig. 2

Make 1 unit,
1½" × 4½".

Fig. 3

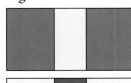

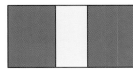

Facets

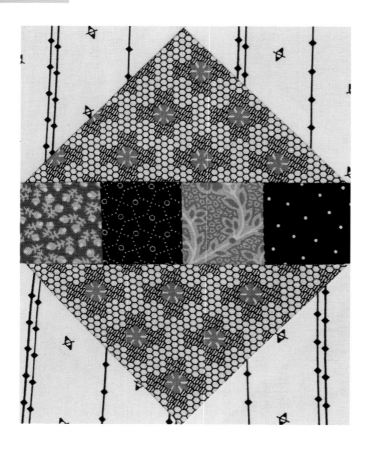

WHAT YOU'LL NEED

☐ **A:** 4 light squares, 2½" × 2½"
▨ **B:** 2 gray rectangles, 2½" × 4½"
▨ **C:** 2 different pink squares, 1½" × 1½"
■ **D:** 2 different black squares, 1½" × 1½"

ASSEMBLY

Press the seam allowances open after sewing each seam unless directed otherwise.

1. Draw a diagonal line from corner to corner on the wrong side of each A square. Referring to "Flying-Geese Units" on page 192, use the marked A squares and the B rectangles to make two flying-geese units.

2. Sew together the C and D squares, alternating the colors (*fig. 1*).

3. Sew the flying-geese units to the top and bottom of the step 2 unit (*fig. 2*).

Fig. 1

Make 1 unit,
1½" × 4½".

Fig. 2

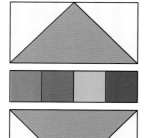

WHAT YOU'LL NEED

- **A:** 6 pink squares, 1½" × 1½"
- **B:** 3 pink rectangles, 1½" × 2"
- **C:** 4 red rectangles, 1" × 1½"
- **D:** 6 red rectangles, 1¼" × 1½"
- **E:** 2 red rectangles, 1" × 2"
- **F:** 4 black rectangles, 1" × 1¼"

ASSEMBLY

Press the seam allowances open after sewing each seam unless directed otherwise.

1. Sew together three A squares and two C rectangles, alternating them. Make two (*fig. 1*).

2. Sew together three D and two F rectangles, alternating them. Make two (*fig. 2*).

3. Sew together the B and E rectangles, alternating them (*fig. 3*).

4. Arrange the units from steps 1–3 as shown (*fig. 4*). Join the units.

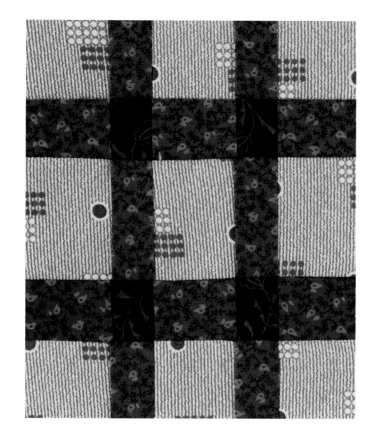

Fig. 1

Make 2 units,
1½" × 4½".

Fig. 2

Make 2 units,
1¼" × 4½".

Fig. 3

Make 1 unit,
2" × 4½".

Fig. 4

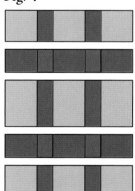

Propeller

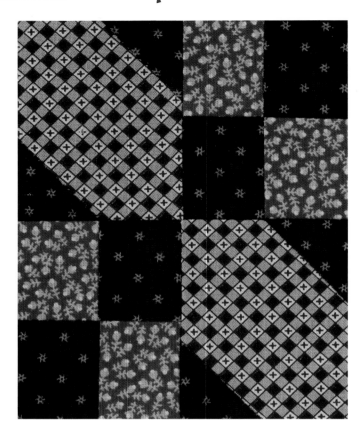

WHAT YOU'LL NEED

A: 4 pink rectangles, 1½" × 1¾"
B: 4 navy rectangles, 1½" × 1¾"
C: 4 navy squares, 1½" × 1½"
D: 2 blue rectangles, 2½" × 3"

ASSEMBLY

Press the seam allowances open after sewing each seam unless directed otherwise.

1. Sew together two A rectangles and two B rectangles in pairs, and then join the pairs. Make two (*fig. 1*).

2. Draw a diagonal line from corner to corner on the wrong side of each C square. Referring to "Stitch-and-Flip Corners" on page 192, join marked C squares to both the upper-right and lower-left corners of a D rectangle. Make two (*fig. 2*).

3. Arrange the units from steps 1 and 2 as shown. Sew the units together into two rows, and then join the rows (*fig. 3*).

Fig. 1

Make 2 units,
2½" × 3".

Fig. 2

Make 2 units,
2½" × 3".

Fig. 3

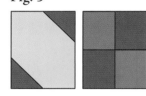

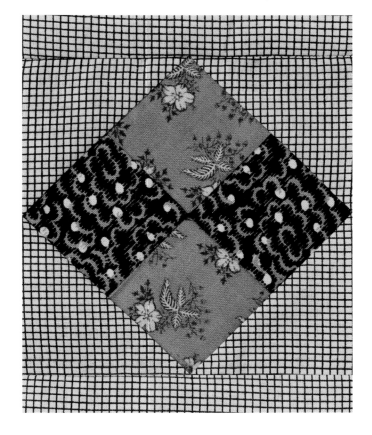

WHAT YOU'LL NEED

- **A:** 2 black squares, 1⅞" × 1⅞"
- **B:** 2 blue squares, 1⅞" × 1⅞"
- **C:** 2 light check squares, 2⅞" × 2⅞"; cut the squares in half diagonally to yield 4 triangles
- **D:** 2 light check rectangles, 1" × 4½"

ASSEMBLY

Press the seam allowances open after sewing each seam unless directed otherwise.

1. Sew together the A and B squares in pairs, and then join the pairs (*fig. 1*).
2. Sew a C triangle to each side of the step 1 unit (*fig. 2*). Press the seam allowances toward the C triangles.
3. Sew the D rectangles to the top and bottom of the step 2 unit (*fig. 3*).

Fig. 1

Make 1 unit,
3¼" × 3¼".

Fig. 2

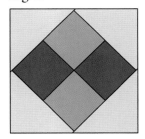

Make 1 unit,
4½" × 4½".

Fig. 3

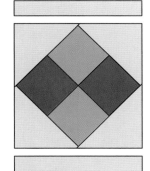

Game Board

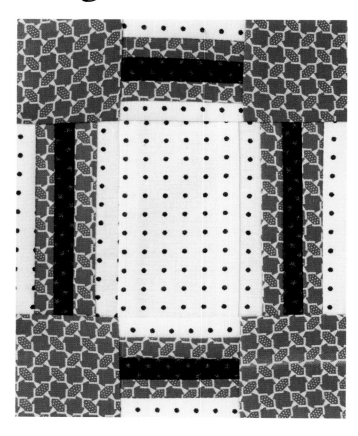

WHAT YOU'LL NEED

- **A:** 2 light strips, ¾" × 12"
- **B:** 1 light rectangle, 2" × 3"
- **C:** 2 red strips, ¾" × 12"
- **D:** 4 red squares, 1¾" × 1¾"
- **E:** 1 black strip, ¾" × 12"

ASSEMBLY

Press the seam allowances open after sewing each seam unless directed otherwise.

1. Sew together the A, C, and E strips to make a strip set. From the strip set, cut two segments measuring 1¾" × 2" and two segments measuring 1¾" × 3" (*fig. 1*).

2. Arrange the step 1 segments, the D squares, and the B rectangle as shown. Sew the pieces together into three rows, and then join the rows (*fig. 2*).

Fig. 1

2" 3"

1¾"

Cut 2 of each segment.

Fig. 2

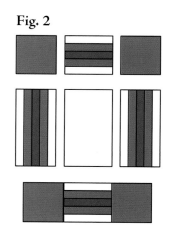

WHAT YOU'LL NEED

 A: 16 assorted light squares, 1" × 1" (4 *each* of 4 different prints)

 B: 16 assorted navy squares, 1" × 1" (4 *each* of 4 different prints)

 **C:** 8 assorted black, pink, and blue rectangles, 1½" × 3"

ASSEMBLY

Press the seam allowances open after sewing each seam unless directed otherwise.

1. Draw a diagonal line from corner to corner on the wrong side of each A square. Referring to "Stitch-and-Flip Corners" on page 192, join matching marked A squares to all four corners of a C rectangle. Make four (*fig. 1*).

2. Draw a diagonal line from corner to corner on the wrong side of each B square. Join matching marked B squares to all four corners of a C rectangle as in step 1. Make four (*fig. 2*).

3. Arrange the units from steps 1 and 2 as shown. Sew the units together into two rows, and then join the rows (*fig. 3*).

Fig. 1

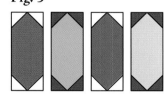

Make 4 units, 1½" × 3".

Fig. 2

Make 4 units, 1½" × 3".

Fig. 3

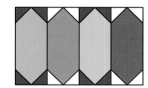

Anniversary

WHAT YOU'LL NEED

 A: 5 pink check squares, 1⅞" × 1⅞"; cut the squares in half diagonally to yield 10 triangles

 B: 2 pink check rectangles, 1½" × 2½"

 C: 2 pink check rectangles, 1½" × 3½"

D: 5 black squares, 1⅞" × 1⅞"; cut the squares in half diagonally to yield 10 triangles

ASSEMBLY

Press the seam allowances open after sewing each seam unless directed otherwise.

1. Referring to "Half-Square-Triangle Units" on page 192, sew the A and D triangles together in pairs to make 10 half-square-triangle units measuring 1½" square. Press the seam allowances toward the D triangles.

2. Arrange six half-square-triangle units as shown. Sew the units together into three rows, and then join the rows (*fig. 1*).

3. Arrange the four remaining half-square-triangle units, the step 2 unit, and the B and C rectangles as shown. Sew the pieces together into three rows, and then join the rows (*fig. 2*).

Fig. 1

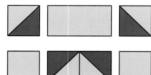

Make 1 unit,
2½" × 3½".

Fig. 2

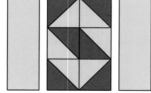

WHAT YOU'LL NEED

A: 4 black #1 squares, 1¼" × 1¼"

B: 2 light rectangles, 2" × 2¼"

C: 2 black #2 rectangles, 2" × 2¼"

D: 2 red #1 rectangles, 1" × 4"

E: 2 red #2 rectangles, 1¼" × 4½"

ASSEMBLY

Press the seam allowances open after sewing each seam unless directed otherwise.

1. Draw a diagonal line from corner to corner on the wrong side of each A square. Referring to "Stitch-and-Flip Corners" on page 192, join a marked A square to the lower-right corner of a B rectangle. Make two. Repeat to join a marked A square to the lower-left corner of a C rectangle, reversing the direction of the sewing line. Make two (*fig. 1*).

2. Sew together the step 1 units in pairs as shown, and then join the pairs (*fig. 2*).

3. Sew the D rectangles to opposite sides of the step 2 unit. Sew the E rectangles to the top and bottom of the unit (*fig. 3*).

Fig. 1

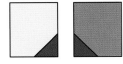

Make 2 of each unit,
2" × 2¼".

Fig. 2

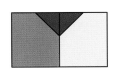

Make 1 unit,
3½" × 4".

Fig. 3

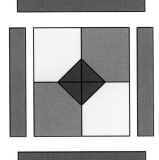

Savannah

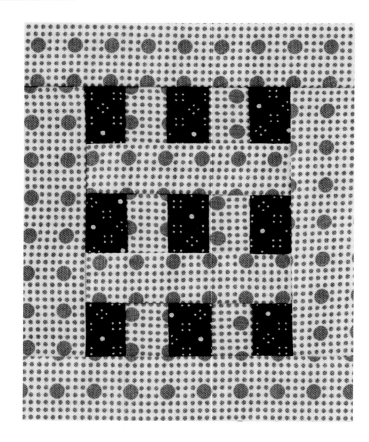

WHAT YOU'LL NEED

A: 9 black rectangles, 1" × 1¼"

B: 6 light rectangles, 1" × 1¼"

C: 2 light rectangles, 1⅛" × 3"

D: 2 light rectangles, 1¼" × 4"

E: 2 light rectangles, 1¼" × 4½"

ASSEMBLY

Press the seam allowances open after sewing each seam unless directed otherwise.

1. Sew together three A and two B rectangles, alternating them. Make three (*fig. 1*).

2. Sew together the step 1 units and the C rectangles as shown (*fig. 2*).

3. Sew the D rectangles to opposite sides of the step 2 unit. Join the E rectangles to the top and bottom of the unit (*fig. 3*).

Fig. 1

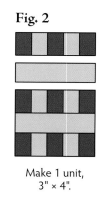

Make 3 units,
1¼" × 3".

Fig. 2

Make 1 unit,
3" × 4".

Fig. 3

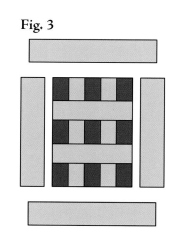

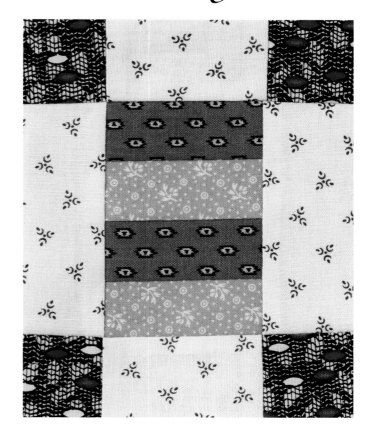

WHAT YOU'LL NEED

- **A:** 2 red rectangles, 1¼" × 2½"
- **B:** 2 pink rectangles, 1¼" × 2½"
- **C:** 2 light rectangles, 1½" × 3½"
- **D:** 2 light rectangles, 1½" × 2½"
- **E:** 4 black squares, 1½" × 1½"

ASSEMBLY

Press the seam allowances open after sewing each seam unless directed otherwise.

1. Sew together the A and B rectangles (*fig. 1*).
2. Arrange the step 1 unit, the E squares, and the D and C rectangles as shown. Sew the pieces together into three rows, and then join the rows (*fig. 2*).

Fig. 1   **Fig. 2**

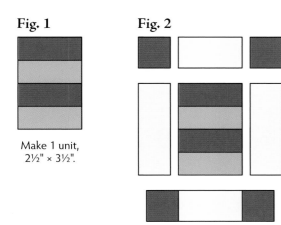

Make 1 unit,
2½" × 3½".

69 *Honeycomb*

WHAT YOU'LL NEED

A: 1 blue stripe rectangle, 2" × 16"
B: 1 pink rectangle, 2" × 4"
C: 1 light rectangle, 4½" × 5½"
10 cardstock templates of the hexagon pattern (below)
    OR 10 precut ⅞" hexagons

ASSEMBLY

1. Using the pattern below and the A and B rectangles, cut eight A hexagons and two B hexagons, adding a ¼" seam allowance to each edge. Baste or glue the seam allowances of each A and B hexagon to the back of a paper template. Make 10 (*fig. 1*).

2. With right sides together, whipstitch the two B hexagons together along one edge. Whipstitch the A hexagons to the remaining edges of the B hexagons, and then whipstitch the A hexagon edges together (*fig. 2*). Carefully press the unit with a pressing cloth, or turn the unit over and press on the wrong side.

3. Center, and then use small whipstitches to appliqué the step 2 unit to the C rectangle. Remove the hexagon papers before you appliqué, or cut away the fabric behind the unit and remove the papers after you appliqué.

Fig. 1

Make 10.

Fig. 2

Hexagon
Cut 10.

Pattern does not include seam allowance.

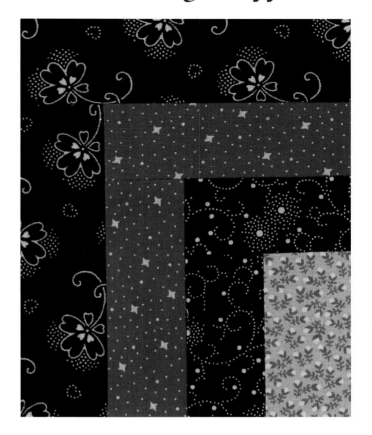

WHAT YOU'LL NEED

A: 1 pink rectangle, 1½" × 2½"
B: 2 black rectangles, 1½" × 2½"
C: 2 red rectangles, 1½" × 3½"
D: 2 blue rectangles, 1½" × 4½"

ASSEMBLY

Press the seam allowances open after sewing each seam unless directed otherwise.

1. Sew a B rectangle to the left side of the A rectangle, then join a B rectangle to the top of the unit (*fig. 1*).
2. Sew a C rectangle to the left side of the step 1 unit, then join a C rectangle to the top of the unit (*fig. 2*).
3. Sew a D rectangle to the left side of the step 2 unit, then join a D rectangle to the top of the unit (*fig. 3*).

Fig. 1

Make 1 unit,
2½" × 3½".

Fig. 2

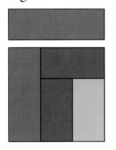

Make 1 unit,
3½" × 4½".

Fig. 3

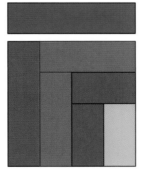

Cousins

WHAT YOU'LL NEED

- **A:** 2 red check rectangles, 1" × 1½"
- **B:** 2 red check squares, 1" × 1"
- **C:** 4 red check squares, 1¼" × 1¼"
- **D:** 2 red check rectangles, 1¼" × 2"
- **E:** 2 red check rectangles, 1¾" × 3"
- **F:** 4 blue rectangles, 1" × 1½"
- **G:** 1 blue square, 1" × 1"
- **H:** 4 blue rectangles, 1" × 1¼"
- **I:** 2 blue rectangles, 1" × 4½"

ASSEMBLY

Press the seam allowances open after sewing each seam unless directed otherwise.

1. Arrange the F and A rectangles and the B and G squares as shown. Sew the pieces together into three rows, and then join the rows (*fig. 1*).

2. Sew the E rectangles to opposite sides of the step 1 unit (*fig. 2*).

3. Sew together two C squares, two H rectangles, and one D rectangle. Make two (*fig. 3*).

4. Arrange the units from steps 2 and 3 and the I rectangles as shown (*fig. 4*). Join the pieces.

Fig. 1

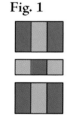

Make 1 unit,
2" × 3".

Fig. 2

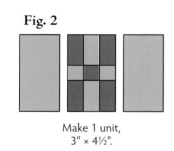

Make 1 unit,
3" × 4½".

Fig. 3

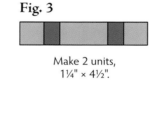

Make 2 units,
1¼" × 4½".

Fig. 4

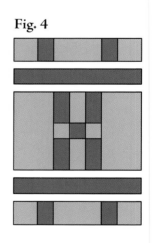

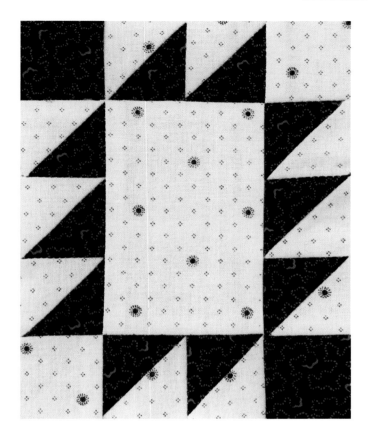

WHAT YOU'LL NEED

☐ **A:** 5 light squares, 1⅞" × 1⅞"; cut the squares in half diagonally to yield 10 triangles

☐ **B:** 2 light squares, 1½" × 1½"

☐ **C:** 1 light rectangle, 2½" × 3½"

■ **D:** 5 black squares, 1⅞" × 1⅞"; cut the squares in half diagonally to yield 10 triangles

■ **E:** 2 black squares, 1½" × 1½"

ASSEMBLY

Press the seam allowances open after sewing each seam unless directed otherwise.

1. Referring to "Half-Square-Triangle Units" on page 192, sew the A and D triangles together in pairs to make 10 half-square-triangle units measuring 1½" square. Press the seam allowances toward the D triangles.

2. Sew together three half-square-triangle units. Make two. Sew these units to opposite sides of the C rectangle (*fig. 1*).

3. Sew together an E square, two half-square-triangle units, and a B square. Make two (*fig. 2*).

4. Sew the step 3 units to the top and bottom of the step 2 unit, noting the color placement (*fig. 3*).

Fig. 1

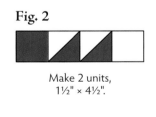

Make 1 unit, 3½" × 4½".

Fig. 2

Make 2 units, 1½" × 4½".

Fig. 3

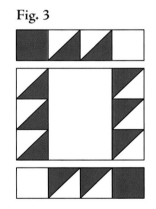

Water Wheel

WHAT YOU'LL NEED

■ **A and B:** 1 red rectangle, 5" × 10"
□ **C and D:** 1 light rectangle, 3" × 10"

ASSEMBLY

Press the seam allowances open after sewing each seam unless directed otherwise.

1. Using the patterns on page 195, and referring to the patchwork template instructions on page 192, cut two A pieces and two B pieces from the red 5" × 10" rectangle. Cut two C triangles and two D triangles from the light 3" × 10" rectangle.

2. Sew together an A piece and a C triangle. Make two (*fig. 1*).

3. Sew together a B piece and a D triangle. Make two (*fig. 2*).

4. Join the units from steps 2 and 3 in pairs as shown, and then sew the pairs together (*fig. 3*).

Fig. 1

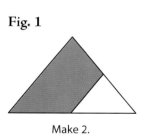

Make 2.

Fig. 2

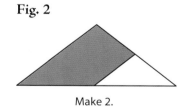

Make 2.

Fig. 3

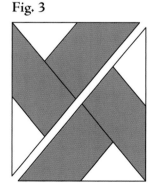

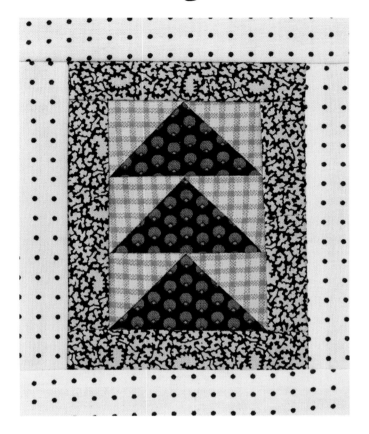

WHAT YOU'LL NEED

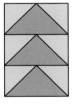 **A:** 6 pink check squares, 1½" × 1½"

B: 3 blue rectangles, 1½" × 2½"

C: 4 black rectangles, 1" × 3½"

D: 4 light rectangles, 1" × 4½"

ASSEMBLY

Press the seam allowances open after sewing each seam unless directed otherwise.

1. Draw a diagonal line from corner to corner on the wrong side of each A square. Referring to "Flying-Geese Units" on page 192, use the marked A squares and the B rectangles to make three flying-geese units. Join the flying-geese units in a vertical row (*fig. 1*).

2. Sew C rectangles to opposite sides of the step 1 unit. Join the remaining C rectangles to the top and bottom of the unit (*fig. 2*).

3. Sew D rectangles to opposite sides of the step 2 unit. Join the remaining D rectangles to the top and bottom of the unit (*fig. 3*).

Fig. 1

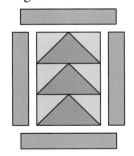

Make 1 unit,
2½" × 3½".

Fig. 2

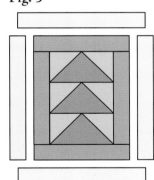

Make 1 unit,
3½" × 4½".

Fig. 3

Confetti

WHAT YOU'LL NEED

■ **A:** 8 assorted red, pink, and black squares, 1½" × 1½"

■ **B:** 2 different red or pink squares, 1⅞" × 1⅞"; cut the squares in half diagonally to yield 4 triangles (you'll have 2 left over)

☐ **C:** 2 different light squares, 1⅞" × 1⅞"; cut the squares in half diagonally to yield 4 triangles (you'll have 2 left over)

☐ **D:** 8 assorted light rectangles, 1½" × 2½"

☐ **E:** 2 different light squares, 1½" × 1½"

ASSEMBLY

Press the seam allowances open after sewing each seam unless directed otherwise.

1. Draw a diagonal line from corner to corner on the wrong side of each A square. Referring to "Stitch-and-Flip Corners" on page 192, join a marked A square to the left end of a D rectangle. Make eight (*fig. 1*).

2. Referring to "Half-Square-Triangle Units" on page 192, sew a B triangle and C triangle together to make a half-square-triangle unit measuring 1½" square. Make two. Press the seam allowances toward the B triangles.

3. Arrange the step 1 units, the half-square-triangle units, and the E squares as shown. Sew the pieces together into five rows, and then join the rows (*fig. 2*).

Fig. 1

Make 8 units,
1½" × 2½".

Fig. 2

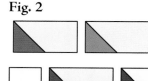

WHAT YOU'LL NEED

☐ **A:** 16 light squares, 1½" × 1½"

▨ **B:** 4 blue rectangles, 1½" × 3"

▧ **C:** 4 pink rectangles, 1½" × 3"

ASSEMBLY

Press the seam allowances open after sewing each seam unless directed otherwise.

1. Draw a diagonal line from corner to corner on the wrong side of each A square.

2. Referring to "Stitch-and-Flip Corners" on page 192, join a marked A square to each end of a B rectangle. Make four (*fig. 1*).

3. Join a marked A square to each end of a C rectangle as in step 2, noting the change in direction of the sewing lines. Make four (*fig. 2*).

4. Arrange the units from steps 2 and 3 as shown. Sew the units together into two rows, and then join the rows (*fig. 3*).

Fig. 1

Make 4 units,
1½" × 3".

Fig. 2

Make 4 units,
1½" × 3".

Fig. 3

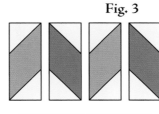

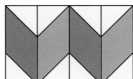

Hopscotch

WHAT YOU'LL NEED

■ **A:** 10 black #1 squares, 1" × 1"
■ **B:** 10 black #2 squares, 1" × 1"
□ **C:** 8 light rectangles, 1" × 1½"
□ **D:** 8 light squares, 1" × 1"
□ **E:** 2 light rectangles, 1½" × 2"
□ **F:** 2 light rectangles, 2" × 2½"

ASSEMBLY

Press the seam allowances open after sewing each seam unless directed otherwise.

1. Join the A and B squares in pairs. Make four. Join the pairs (*fig. 1*). Trim all seam allowances to ⅛".

2. Arrange two A squares, two C rectangles, two D squares, and one B square as shown. Sew the pieces together into three vertical rows, and then join the rows. Make two (*fig. 2*).

3. Arrange two C rectangles, two B squares, two D squares, and one A square as shown. Sew the pieces together into three horizontal rows, and then join the rows. Make two (*fig. 3*).

4. Arrange the units from steps 1–3 and the E and F rectangles as shown. Sew the pieces together into three rows, and then join the rows (*fig. 4*).

Fig. 1

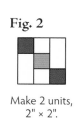

Make 1 unit,
1½" × 2½".

Fig. 2

Make 2 units,
2" × 2".

Fig. 3

Make 2 units,
2" × 2".

Fig. 4

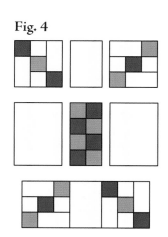

WHAT YOU'LL NEED

 A: 2 light squares, 2⅛" × 2⅛"; cut the squares in half diagonally to yield 4 triangles

B: 4 light rectangles, 1⅛" × 1¼"

C: 4 light rectangles, 1⅛" × 1¾"

D: 1 light rectangle, 2" × 3"

E: 2 black squares, 2⅛" × 2⅛"; cut the squares in half diagonally to yield 4 triangles

F: 4 black rectangles, 1⅛" × 1¼"

G: 4 black rectangles, 1⅛" × 1¾"

ASSEMBLY

Press the seam allowances open after sewing each seam unless directed otherwise.

1. Referring to "Half-Square-Triangle Units" on page 192, sew the A and E triangles together in pairs to make four half-square-triangle units measuring 1¾" square. Press the seam allowances toward the E triangles.

2. Sew together two B rectangles and two F rectangles in pairs, and then join the pairs. Make two (*fig. 1*).

3. Sew together two C rectangles and two G rectangles in pairs, and then join the pairs. Make two (*fig. 2*).

4. Arrange the units from steps 1–3 and the D rectangle as shown. Sew the pieces together into three rows, and then join the rows (*fig. 3*).

Fig. 1

Make 2 units,
1¾" × 2".

Fig. 2

Make 2 units,
1¾" × 3".

Fig. 3

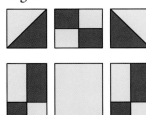

Lacewing

WHAT YOU'LL NEED

☐ **A:** 1 light rectangle, 5" × 6"

▨ **B and C:** 1 red check rectangle, 6" × 7"

■ **D:** 1 red rectangle, 5" × 8"

ASSEMBLY

Press the seam allowances open after sewing each seam unless directed otherwise.

1. Using the patterns on page 196, and referring to the patchwork and appliqué template instructions on page 192, cut one A diamond from the light 5" × 6" rectangle, two B and two B reversed triangles from the red check 6" × 7" rectangle, and four C pieces from the red 5" × 8" rectangle. Prepare the C pieces for your preferred appliqué method.

2. Sew the B triangles to the upper-left and lower-right sides of A. Join the B reversed triangles to the upper-right and lower-left sides of A (*fig. 1*).

3. Referring to the photo for guidance, position the C pieces on the step 2 unit, with the points meeting in the center of A. Pin or baste them in place.

4. Use your preferred appliqué method to sew the C pieces in place. Carefully press the block with a pressing cloth, or turn the block over and press on the wrong side.

Fig. 1

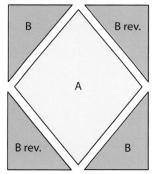

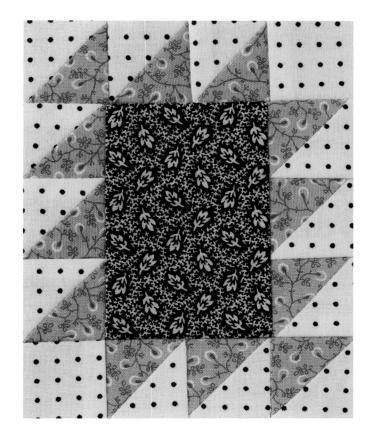

WHAT YOU'LL NEED

A: 6 light squares, 1⅞" × 1⅞"; cut the squares in half diagonally to yield 12 triangles

B: 2 light squares, 1½" × 1½"

C: 6 pink squares, 1⅞" × 1⅞"; cut the squares in half diagonally to yield 12 triangles

D: 1 black rectangle, 2½" × 3½"

ASSEMBLY

Press the seam allowances open after sewing each seam unless directed otherwise.

1. Referring to "Half-Square-Triangle Units" on page 192, sew the A and C triangles together in pairs to make 12 half-square-triangle units measuring 1½" square. Press the seam allowances toward the C triangles.

2. Sew together three half-square-triangle units. Make two. Sew these units to opposite sides of the D rectangle (*fig. 1*).

3. Join three half-square-triangle units and one B square. Make two (*fig. 2*).

4. Sew the step 3 units to the top and bottom of the step 2 unit as shown (*fig. 3*).

Fig. 1

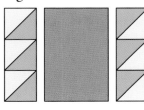

Make 1 unit,
3½" × 4½".

Fig. 2

Make 2 units,
1½" × 4½".

Fig. 3

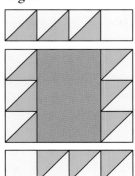

Cherry-O

WHAT YOU'LL NEED

☐ **A:** 2 light squares, 1⅞" × 1⅞"; cut the squares in half diagonally to yield 4 triangles

☐ **B:** 1 light square, 1½" × 1½"

◩ **C:** 2 red #1 squares, 1⅞" × 1⅞"; cut the squares in half diagonally to yield 4 triangles

■ **D:** 4 red #2 squares, 1½" × 1½"

■ **E:** 4 navy rectangles, 1" × 3"

■ **F:** 3 navy rectangles, 1" × 1½"

■ **G:** 4 gray rectangles, 1" × 3"

■ **H:** 3 gray rectangles, 1" × 1½"

ASSEMBLY

Press the seam allowances open after sewing each seam unless directed otherwise.

1. Referring to "Half-Square-Triangle Units" on page 192, sew the A and C triangles together in pairs to make four half-square-triangle units measuring 1½" square. Press the seam allowances toward the C triangles.

2. Arrange the half-square-triangle units and the D and B squares as shown. Sew the pieces together into three rows, and then join the rows (*fig. 1*).

3. Sew together the E and G rectangles. Cut this unit in half to make two 1½" × 4½" segments (*fig. 2*).

4. Join two H rectangles and one F rectangle; sew this unit to the left side of the step 2 unit. Join two F rectangles and one H rectangle; sew this unit to the right side of the step 2 unit (*fig. 3*).

5. Sew the step 3 segments to the top and bottom of the step 4 unit (*fig. 4*).

Fig. 1

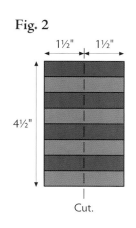

Make 1 unit,
3½" × 3½".

Fig. 2

1½"   1½"

4½"

Cut.

Fig. 3

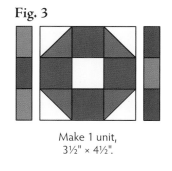

Make 1 unit,
3½" × 4½".

Fig. 4

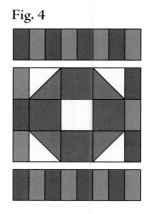

WHAT YOU'LL NEED

☐ **A:** 14 light squares, 1½" × 1½"
☐ **B:** 3 light rectangles, 1½" × 2½"
▨ **C:** 5 assorted blue rectangles, 1½" × 2½"

ASSEMBLY

Press the seam allowances open after sewing each seam unless directed otherwise.

1. Draw a diagonal line from corner to corner on the wrong side of 10 A squares. Referring to "Flying-Geese Units" on page 192, use the marked A squares and the C rectangles to make five flying-geese units.

2. Arrange the flying-geese units, the four remaining A squares, and the B rectangles as shown. Sew the pieces together into five rows, and then join the rows (*fig. 1*).

Fig. 1

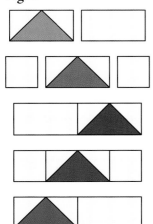

Four Rectangles

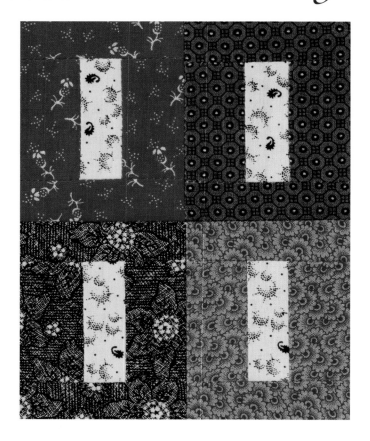

WHAT YOU'LL NEED

☐ **A:** 4 light rectangles, 1" × 2"
■ **B:** 2 red rectangles, 1¼" × 2"
■ **C:** 2 red rectangles, 1" × 2½"
■ **D:** 2 blue rectangles, 1¼" × 2"
■ **E:** 2 blue rectangles, 1" × 2½"
■ **F:** 2 black rectangles, 1¼" × 2"
■ **G:** 2 black rectangles, 1" × 2½"
■ **H:** 2 pink rectangles, 1¼" × 2"
■ **I:** 2 pink rectangles, 1" × 2½"

ASSEMBLY

Press the seam allowances open after sewing each seam unless directed otherwise.

1. Sew together two B rectangles and an A rectangle. Join the C rectangles to the top and bottom of the unit (*fig. 1*). Repeat to make blue, black, and pink units using the D–I rectangles.

2. Sew the step 1 units together into two rows as shown, and then join the rows (*fig. 2*).

Fig. 1

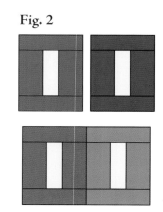

Make 4 units,
2½" × 3".

Fig. 2

WHAT YOU'LL NEED

A: 10 pink squares, 1½" × 1½"

B: 3 assorted burgundy rectangles, 1½" × 4½"

C: 2 blue rectangles, 1½" × 2½"

ASSEMBLY

Press the seam allowances open after sewing each seam unless directed otherwise.

1. Draw a diagonal line from corner to corner on the wrong side of six A squares. Referring to "Stitch-and-Flip Corners" on page 192, join a marked A square to each end of a B rectangle. Make three (*fig. 1*).

2. Sew an A square to each end of a C rectangle. Make two (*fig. 2*).

3. Arrange the units from steps 1 and 2 as shown (*fig. 3*). Join the units.

Fig. 1

Make 3 units,
1½" × 4½".

Fig. 2

Make 2 units,
1½" × 4½".

Fig. 3

Red Cross

WHAT YOU'LL NEED

☐ **A:** 2 light rectangles, 1½" × 2½"
☐ **B:** 4 light rectangles, 1½" × 2"
☐ **C:** 2 light rectangles, 1" × 1½"
▣ **D:** 6 red squares, 1½" × 1½"
▣ **E:** 1 red rectangle, 1½" × 3½"

ASSEMBLY

Press the seam allowances open after sewing each seam unless directed otherwise.

1. Sew a D square to each end of an A rectangle. Make two (*fig. 1*).

2. Sew a B rectangle to opposite sides of a D square. Make two (*fig. 2*).

3. Sew the C rectangles to each end of the E rectangle (*fig. 3*).

4. Arrange the units from steps 1–3 as shown (*fig. 4*). Join the units.

Fig. 1

Make 2 units,
1½" × 4½".

Fig. 2

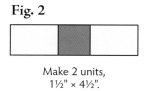

Make 2 units,
1½" × 4½".

Fig. 3

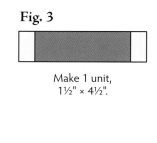

Make 1 unit,
1½" × 4½".

Fig. 4

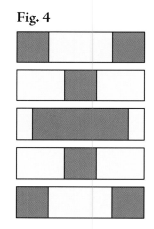

WHAT YOU'LL NEED

- **A:** 2 light rectangles, ¾" × 1½"
- **B:** 2 light rectangles, ¾" × 3"
- **C:** 10 light squares, 1" × 1"
- **D:** 2 light rectangles, 1¼" × 4"
- **E:** 2 light rectangles, 1¼" × 4½"
- **F:** 10 pink squares, 1" × 1"
- **G:** 1 navy rectangle, 1½" × 2½"

ASSEMBLY

Press the seam allowances open after sewing each seam unless directed otherwise.

1. Sew the A rectangles to the top and bottom of the G rectangle. Join the B rectangles to opposite sides of the unit (*fig. 1*). Trim the seam allowances to ⅛".

2. Sew together three F squares and two C squares, alternating them; trim as in step 1. Make two (*fig. 2*).

3. Sew together three C squares and two F squares, alternating them; trim as in step 1. Make two (*fig. 3*).

4. Sew the step 2 units to opposite sides of the step 1 unit. Join the step 3 units to the top and bottom of the unit (*fig. 4*). Trim as in step 1.

5. Sew the D rectangles to opposite sides of the step 4 unit. Sew the E rectangles to the top and bottom of the unit (*fig. 5*).

Fig. 1

Make 1 unit,
2" × 3".

Fig. 2

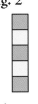

Make 2 units,
1" × 3".

Fig. 3

Make 2 units,
1" × 3".

Fig. 4

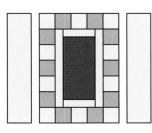

Make 1 unit,
3" × 4".

Fig. 5

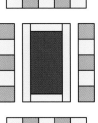

Good Night

WHAT YOU'LL NEED

■ **A:** 4 blue rectangles, 1¾" × 2¼"

□ **B:** 2 light rectangles, 1" × 2¼"

□ **C:** 1 light rectangle, 1" × 3½"

■ **D:** 4 black rectangles, 1" × 4½"

ASSEMBLY

Press the seam allowances open after sewing each seam unless directed otherwise.

1. Arrange the A, B, and C rectangles in three rows as shown. Join the pieces in the top and bottom rows, and then join the rows (*fig. 1*).

2. Sew D rectangles to opposite sides of the step 1 unit. Join the remaining D rectangles to the top and bottom of the unit (*fig. 2*).

Fig. 1 **Fig. 2**

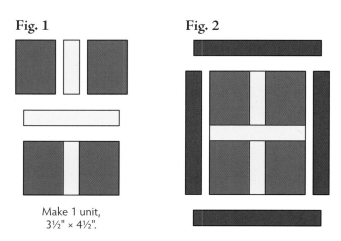

Make 1 unit,
3½" × 4½".

WHAT YOU'LL NEED

A: 4 gray rectangles, 1½" × 2"

B: 4 gray rectangles, 1¼" × 1½"

C: 1 gray square, 1½" × 1½"

D: 2 red squares, 1½" × 1½"

E: 6 red rectangles, 1¼" × 1½"

F: 2 pink squares, 1½" × 1½"

G: 2 pink rectangles, 1¼" × 1½"

ASSEMBLY

Press the seam allowances open after sewing each seam unless directed otherwise.

1. Sew an A rectangle to opposite sides of a D square. Make two (*fig. 1*).

2. Sew together two B rectangles, two E rectangles, and an F square as shown (*fig. 2*). Make two.

3. Sew together two E rectangles, the G rectangles, and the C square as shown (*fig. 3*).

4. Arrange the units from steps 1–3 as shown (*fig. 4*). Join the units.

Fig. 1

Make 2 units,
1½" × 4½".

Fig. 2

Make 2 units,
1½" × 4½".

Fig. 3

Make 1 unit,
1½" × 4½".

Fig. 4

Spinning Spools

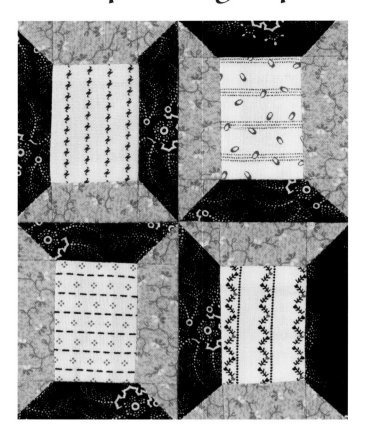

WHAT YOU'LL NEED

▪ **A:** 4 black rectangles, 1" × 3"

▪ **B:** 4 black rectangles, 1" × 2½"

▫ **C:** 16 pink squares, 1" × 1"

▫ **D:** 4 pink rectangles, 1" × 1½"

▫ **E:** 4 pink rectangles, 1" × 2"

▫ **F:** 4 assorted light stripe rectangles, 1½" × 2"

ASSEMBLY

Press the seam allowances open after sewing each seam unless directed otherwise.

1. Draw a diagonal line from corner to corner on the wrong side of each C square. Referring to "Stitch-and-Flip Corners" on page 192, join a marked C square to each end of an A rectangle. Make four (*fig. 1*).

2. Join D rectangles to the top and bottom of an F rectangle. Sew step 1 units to opposite sides of the unit. Make two (*fig. 2*).

3. Join a marked C square to each end of a B rectangle as in step 1. Make four.

4. Join E rectangles to opposite sides of an F rectangle. Sew step 3 units to the top and bottom of the unit. Make two (*fig. 3*).

5. Arrange the units from steps 2 and 4 as shown. Sew the units together into two rows, and then join the rows (*fig. 4*).

Fig. 1

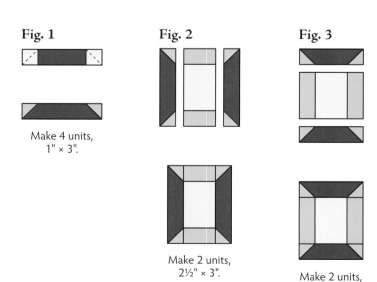

Make 4 units, 1" × 3".

Fig. 2

Make 2 units, 2½" × 3".

Fig. 3

Make 2 units, 2½" × 3".

Fig. 4

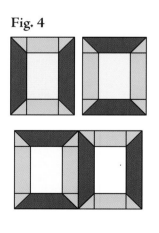

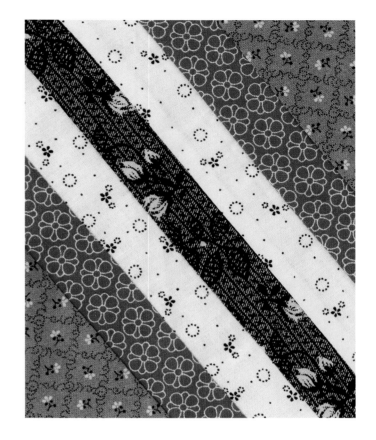

WHAT YOU'LL NEED

■ **Position 1:** 1 black scrap, about 1½" × 8"

□ **Positions 2 and 5:** 2 cream scraps, about 1½" × 6"

■ **Positions 3 and 6:** 2 red scraps, about 1½" × 7"

■ **Positions 4 and 7:** 2 blue scraps, about 3½" × 3½"

1 photocopy or tracing of the Slant paper-foundation
     piecing pattern (page 197)

ASSEMBLY

1. Using the prepared pattern and the black, cream,
   red, and blue scraps, paper piece the block. Refer
   to the photo and the illustrated, downloadable
   Paper-Foundation Piecing tutorial at
   ShopMartingale.com/HowtoQuilt as needed.

2. Press the block with a medium-hot iron, and then
   remove the foundation paper.

Hot Cross Buns

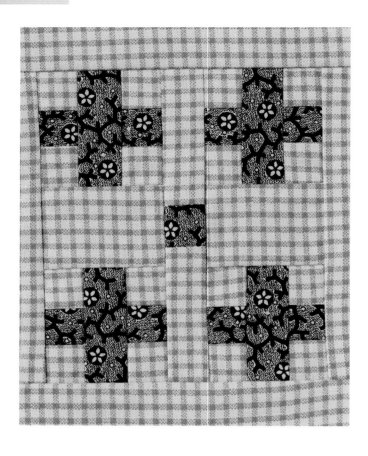

WHAT YOU'LL NEED

A: 16 light check squares, 1" × 1"

B: 2 light check rectangles 1½" × 2"

C: 2 light check rectangles, 1" × 2¼"

D: 2 light check rectangles, ¾" × 4½"

E: 2 light check rectangles, 1" × 4½"

F: 9 black squares, 1" × 1"

G: 4 black rectangles, 1" × 2"

ASSEMBLY

Press the seam allowances open after sewing each seam unless directed otherwise.

1. Arrange four A squares, two F squares, and one G rectangle in three vertical rows as shown. Sew together the squares in the left and right rows, and then join the rows. Make four (*fig. 1*).

2. Lay out the step 1 units, the B and C rectangles, and the remaining F square as shown. Sew the pieces together into three rows, and then join the rows (*fig. 2*).

3. Sew the D rectangles to opposite sides of the step 2 unit. Join the E rectangles to the top and bottom of the unit (*fig. 3*).

Fig. 1

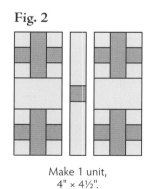

Make 4 units,
2" × 2".

Fig. 2

Make 1 unit,
4" × 4½".

Fig. 3

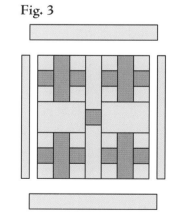

WHAT YOU'LL NEED

A: 4 red rectangles, 1" × 1½"

B: 4 red rectangles, 1" × 3"

C: 2 black rectangles, 1½" × 2"

D: 2 light plaid rectangles, 2½" × 3"

ASSEMBLY

Press the seam allowances open after sewing each seam unless directed otherwise.

1. Sew A rectangles to the top and bottom of a C rectangle. Make two (*fig. 1*).

2. Join B rectangles to opposite sides of a step 1 unit. Make two (*fig. 2*).

3. Arrange the step 2 units and the D rectangles as shown. Sew the pieces together into two rows, and then join the rows (*fig. 3*).

Fig. 1

Make 2 units, 1½" × 3".

Fig. 2

Make 2 units, 2½" × 3".

Fig. 3

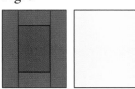

Formation

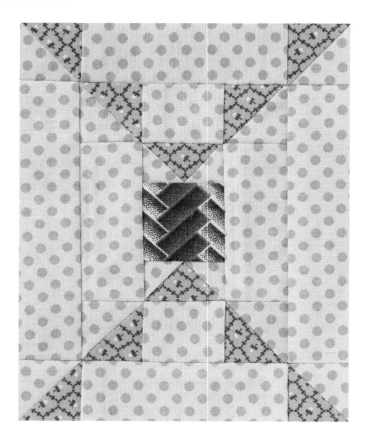

WHAT YOU'LL NEED

☐ **A:** 4 light squares, 1" × 1"

☐ **B:** 4 light squares, 1⅝" × 1⅝"; cut the squares in half diagonally to yield 8 triangles

☐ **C:** 2 light rectangles, 1¼" × 2½"

☐ **D:** 2 light rectangles, 1¼" × 1½"

☐ **E:** 2 light rectangles, 1¼" × 4"

☐ **F:** 2 light rectangles, 1¼" × 3"

☐ **G:** 2 pink rectangles, 1" × 1½"

☐ **H:** 4 pink squares, 1⅝" × 1⅝"; cut the squares in half diagonally to yield 8 triangles

☐ **I:** 1 blue square, 1½" × 1½"

ASSEMBLY

Press the seam allowances open after sewing each seam unless directed otherwise.

1. Draw a diagonal line from corner to corner on the wrong side of each A square. Referring to "Flying-Geese Units" on page 192, use the marked A squares and the G rectangles to make two flying-geese units. Sew the flying-geese units to the top and bottom of the I square (*fig. 1*).

2. Referring to "Half-Square-Triangle Units" on page 192, sew the B and H triangles together in pairs to make eight half-square-triangle units measuring 1¼" square. Press the seam allowances toward the H triangles.

3. Arrange the step 1 unit, four half-square-triangle units, and the D and C rectangles as shown. Sew the pieces together into three rows, and then join the rows (*fig. 2*).

4. Arrange the step 3 unit, four half-square-triangle units, and the F and E rectangles as shown. Sew the pieces together into three rows, and then join the rows (*fig. 3*).

Fig. 1

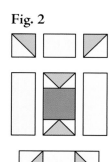

Make 1 unit,
1½" × 2½".

Fig. 2

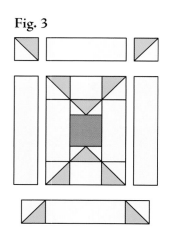

Make 1 unit,
3" × 4".

Fig. 3

WHAT YOU'LL NEED

 A: 2 light rectangles, 1½" × 4"

 B: 3 light squares, 2¼" × 2¼"; cut the squares into quarters diagonally to yield 12 triangles (you'll have 2 left over)

C: 3 blue rectangles, 1½" × 4"

D: 3 blue squares, 2¼" × 2¼"; cut the squares into quarters diagonally to yield 12 triangles (you'll have 2 left over)

ASSEMBLY

Press the seam allowances open after sewing each seam unless directed otherwise.

1. Sew together two B triangles and two D triangles in pairs as shown. Join the pairs to make a quarter-square-triangle unit measuring 1½" square. Make five (*fig. 1*).

2. Sew together the C and A rectangles. Cut this unit in half vertically to make two 2" × 5½" segments (*fig. 2*).

3. Join the quarter-square-triangle units in a vertical row as shown. Sew the step 2 segments to opposite sides of the row (*fig. 3*).

Fig. 1

Fig. 2

Fig. 3

Make 5 units,
1½" × 1½".

2"   2"

5½"

Cut.

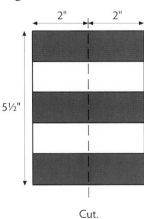

Stellar

WHAT YOU'LL NEED

A: 4 light rectangles, 1½" × 2½"

B: 2 light squares, 1⅞" × 1⅞"; cut the squares in half diagonally to yield 4 triangles

C: 2 light rectangles, 1" × 4½"

D: 8 pink squares, 1½" × 1½"

E: 2 pink squares, 1⅞" × 1⅞"; cut the squares in half diagonally to yield 4 triangles

F: 1 blue square, 2½" × 2½"

ASSEMBLY

Press the seam allowances open after sewing each seam unless directed otherwise.

1. Draw a diagonal line from corner to corner on the wrong side of each D square. Referring to "Flying-Geese Units" on page 192, use the marked D squares and the A rectangles to make four flying-geese units.

2. Referring to "Half-Square-Triangle Units" on page 192, sew the B and E triangles together in pairs to make four half-square-triangle units measuring 1½" square. Press the seam allowances toward the E triangles.

3. Arrange the flying-geese units, the half-square-triangle units, and the F square as shown. Sew the pieces together into three rows, and then join the rows (*fig. 1*).

4. Sew the C rectangles to the top and bottom of the step 3 unit (*fig. 2*).

Fig. 1

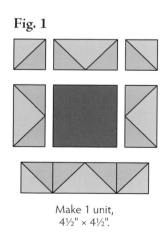

Make 1 unit,
4½" × 4½".

Fig. 2

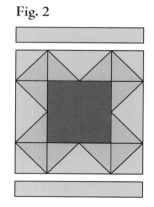

WHAT YOU'LL NEED

- **A:** 2 different red rectangles, 1½" × 3½"
- **B:** 2 different black rectangles, 1½" × 3½"
- **C:** 1 light square, 1½" × 1½"
- **D:** 4 light squares, 1⅞" × 1⅞"; cut the squares in half diagonally to yield 8 triangles (you'll have 1 left over)
- **E:** 4 black dot squares, 1⅞" × 1⅞"; cut the squares in half diagonally to yield 8 triangles (you'll have 1 left over)

ASSEMBLY

Press the seam allowances open after sewing each seam unless directed otherwise.

1. Referring to "Half-Square-Triangle Units" on page 192, sew the D and E triangles together in pairs to make seven half-square-triangle units measuring 1½" square. Press the seam allowances toward the E triangles.

2. Arrange the A and B rectangles and four half-square-triangle units as shown. Sew the pieces together into two vertical rows, and then join the rows (*fig. 1*).

3. Sew together three half-square-triangle units and the C square. Sew this unit to the top of the step 2 unit (*fig. 2*).

Fig. 1

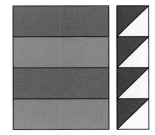

Make 1 unit,
4½" × 4½".

Fig. 2

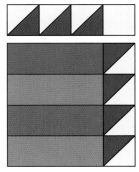

Double Spot

WHAT YOU'LL NEED

- **A:** 1 light #1 rectangle, 1¼" × 1¾"
- **B:** 1 light #1 rectangle, 2¼" × 2½"
- **C:** 1 light #2 rectangle, 1¼" × 1¾"
- **D:** 1 light #2 rectangle, 2¼" × 2½"
- **E:** 1 red square, 1¼" × 1¼"
- **F:** 1 navy square, 1¼" × 1¼"
- **G:** 1 blue check rectangle, 2½" × 3"
- **H:** 1 pink stripe rectangle, 2½" × 3"

ASSEMBLY

Press the seam allowances open after sewing each seam unless directed otherwise.

1. Sew together the E square and the A rectangle. Join the B rectangle to the top edge of the unit (*fig. 1*).

2. Join the C rectangle and the F square. Sew the D rectangle to the bottom edge of the unit (*fig. 2*).

3. Arrange the units from steps 1 and 2 and the G and H rectangles as shown. Sew the pieces together into two rows, and then join the rows (*fig. 3*).

Fig. 1

Make 1 unit,
2½" × 3".

Fig. 2

Make 1 unit,
2½" × 3".

Fig. 3

WHAT YOU'LL NEED

☐ **A:** 4 light squares, 1⅞" × 1⅞"; cut the squares in half diagonally to yield 8 triangles

☐ **B:** 4 light rectangles, 1" × 4½"

▨ **C:** 4 red squares, 1⅞" × 1⅞"; cut the squares in half diagonally to yield 8 triangles

■ **D:** 1 blue rectangle, 1½" × 4½"

ASSEMBLY

Press the seam allowances open after sewing each seam unless directed otherwise.

1. Referring to "Half-Square-Triangle Units" on page 192, sew the A and C triangles together in pairs to make eight half-square-triangle units measuring 1½" square. Press the seam allowances toward the C triangles.

2. Join the half-square-triangle units in two rows of four units each, noting the change in seam directions (*fig. 1*).

3. Sew the step 2 units to opposite sides of the D rectangle (*fig. 2*).

4. Sew B rectangles to opposite sides of the step 3 unit. Join the remaining B rectangles to the top and bottom of the unit (*fig. 3*).

Fig. 1

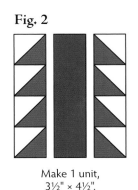

Make 1 of each unit,
1½" × 4½".

Fig. 2

Make 1 unit,
3½" × 4½".

Fig. 3

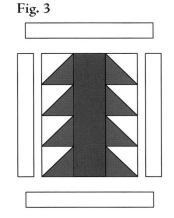

Braid

WHAT YOU'LL NEED

■ **Positions 1–15:** 15 assorted blue scraps, about 1½" × 3½"

□ **A:** 4 light rectangles, 1" × 4½"

1 photocopy or tracing of the Braid paper-foundation piecing pattern (page 196)

ASSEMBLY

1. Using the prepared pattern and the assorted blue scraps, paper piece the block center. Refer to the photo and see the illustrated, downloadable Paper-Foundation Piecing tutorial at ShopMartingale.com/HowtoQuilt as needed.

2. Press the block center with a medium-hot iron, and then remove the foundation paper.

3. Sew A rectangles to opposite sides of the block center. Join the remaining A rectangles to the top and bottom of the unit (*fig. 1*). Press the seam allowances open.

Fig. 1

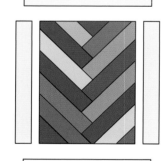

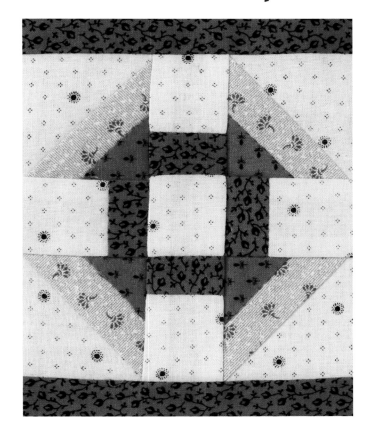

WHAT YOU'LL NEED

- ☐ **A:** 2 light squares, 2⅜" × 2⅜"; cut the squares in half diagonally to yield 4 triangles
- ☐ **B:** 5 light squares, 1½" × 1½"
- ☐ **C:** 2 pink squares, 2⅜" × 2⅜"; cut the squares in half diagonally to yield 4 triangles
- ☐ **D:** 4 red #1 squares, 1¼" × 1¼"
- ☐ **E:** 4 red #2 rectangles, 1" × 1½"
- ☐ **F:** 2 red #2 rectangles, 1" × 4½"

ASSEMBLY

Press the seam allowances open after sewing each seam unless directed otherwise.

1. Referring to "Half-Square-Triangle Units" on page 192, sew the A and C triangles together in pairs to make four half-square-triangle units measuring 2" square. Press the seam allowances toward the C triangles.

2. Draw a diagonal line from corner to corner on the wrong side of each D square. Referring to "Stitch-and-Flip Corners" on page 192, join a marked D square to the pink corner of a half-square-triangle unit. Make four (*fig. 1*).

3. Sew together a B square and an E rectangle. Make four (*fig. 2*).

4. Arrange the units from steps 2 and 3 and the remaining B square as shown. Sew the pieces together into three rows, and then join the rows (*fig. 3*).

5. Sew the F rectangles to the top and bottom of the step 4 unit (*fig. 4*).

Fig. 1

Make 4 units,
2" × 2".

Fig. 2

Make 4 units,
1½" × 2".

Fig. 3

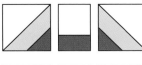

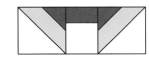

Make 1 unit,
4½" × 4½".

Fig. 4

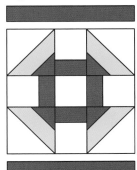

WHAT YOU'LL NEED

■ **A:** 4 black squares, 1" × 1"

■ **B:** 2 black rectangles, 1" × 1½"

■ **C:** 4 black rectangles, 1½" × 1¾"

■ **D:** 2 black rectangles, 1" × 2"

■ **E:** 1 black rectangle, 1½" × 2"

□ **F:** 4 light rectangles, 1" × 1½"

□ **G:** 4 light rectangles, 1" × 1¾"

□ **H:** 2 light rectangles, 1½" × 1¾"

□ **I:** 2 light rectangles, 1½" × 2"

ASSEMBLY

Press the seam allowances open after sewing each seam unless directed otherwise.

1. Sew together two A squares, two F rectangles, and one B rectangle as shown. Make two (*fig. 1*).

2. Sew together two G rectangles, two C rectangles, and one H rectangle as shown. Make two (*fig. 2*).

3. Sew together the D, I, and E rectangles as shown (*fig. 3*).

4. Arrange the units from steps 1–3 as shown (*fig. 4*). Join the units.

Fig. 1

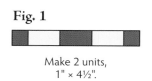

Make 2 units,
1" × 4½".

Fig. 2

Make 2 units,
1¾" × 4½".

Fig. 3

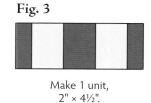

Make 1 unit,
2" × 4½".

Fig. 4

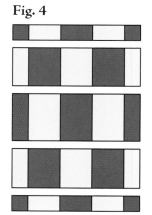

WHAT YOU'LL NEED

A: 8 rectangles, 1½" × 2½" (2 *each* of light blue, red, black, and pink)

B: 16 squares, 1½" × 1½" (4 *each* of red, black, pink, and navy)

C: 5 squares, 1⅞" × 1⅞" (1 *each* of light blue, red, black, pink, and navy); cut the squares in half diagonally to yield 10 triangles (you'll have 1 light blue triangle and 1 navy triangle left over)

ASSEMBLY

Press the seam allowances open after sewing each seam unless directed otherwise.

1. Draw a diagonal line from corner to corner on the wrong side of each B square. Referring to "Flying-Geese Units" on page 192, use the marked B squares and the A rectangles to make a total of eight flying-geese units, two units in *each* of the following color combinations (*fig. 1*):
   + Red B squares and light blue A rectangles
   + Black B squares and red A rectangles
   + Pink B squares and black A rectangles
   + Navy B squares and pink A rectangles

2. Referring to "Half-Square-Triangle Units" on page 192, sew the C triangles together in pairs to make four half-square-triangle units measuring 1½" square, one unit in *each* of the following color combinations (*fig. 2*):
   + Light blue and red C triangles
   + Red and black C triangles
   + Black and pink C triangles
   + Pink and navy C triangles

3. Arrange the flying-geese units and half-square-triangle units in the color sequence shown. Sew the units together into three rows, and then join the rows (*fig. 3*).

Fig. 1

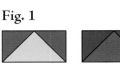

Make 2 of each unit, 1½" × 2½".

Fig. 2

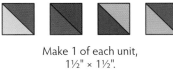

Make 1 of each unit, 1½" × 1½".

Fig. 3

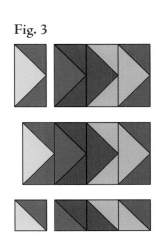

Bar Bells

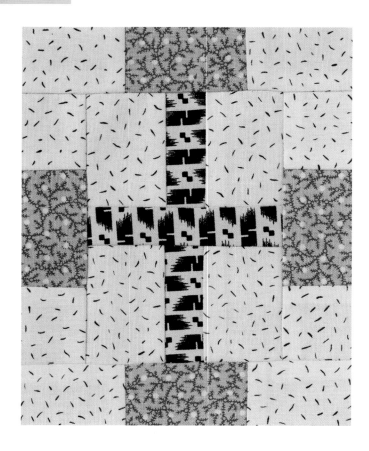

WHAT YOU'LL NEED

- ☐ **A:** 4 light rectangles, 1½" × 2"
- ☐ **B:** 4 light rectangles, 1¼" × 1½"
- ☐ **C:** 4 light rectangles, 1¼" × 1¾"
- ☐ **D:** 2 black rectangles, 1" × 2"
- ☐ **E:** 1 black rectangle, 1" × 3"
- ☐ **F:** 4 pink rectangles, 1¼" × 2"

ASSEMBLY

Press the seam allowances open after sewing each seam unless directed otherwise.

1. Arrange the A, D, and E rectangles in three rows as shown. Join the pieces in the top and bottom rows, and then sew the rows together (*fig. 1*).

2. Sew a B rectangle to each end of an F rectangle. Make two. Join these units to opposite sides of the step 1 unit (*fig. 2*).

3. Sew a C rectangle to each end of an F rectangle. Make two. Join these units to the top and bottom of the step 2 unit (*fig. 3*).

Fig. 1

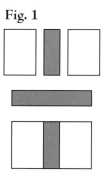

Make 1 unit,
3" × 4".

Fig. 2

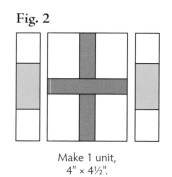

Make 1 unit,
4" × 4½".

Fig. 3

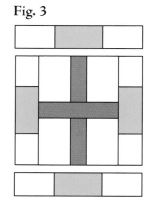

WHAT YOU'LL NEED

- **A:** 6 light squares, 1" × 1"
- **B:** 6 light rectangles, ⅞" × 2"
- **C:** 1 burgundy rectangle, 1" × 1½"
- **D:** 1 burgundy rectangle, ¾" × 2"
- **E:** 1 pink rectangle, 1" × 1½"
- **F:** 1 pink rectangle, ¾" × 2"
- **G:** 1 navy rectangle, 1" × 1½"
- **H:** 1 navy rectangle, ¾" × 2"
- **I:** 2 blue rectangles, 1½" × 2½"
- **J:** 2 blue rectangles, 1½" × 5½"

ASSEMBLY

Press the seam allowances open after sewing each seam unless directed otherwise.

1. Draw a diagonal line from corner to corner on the wrong side of each A square. Referring to "Flying-Geese Units" on page 192, use the marked A squares and the C, E, and G rectangles to make three flying-geese units, one *each* of red, pink, and navy (*fig. 1*).

2. Sew B rectangles to opposite sides of the D, F, and H rectangles. Trim the seam allowances to ⅛". Join a matching flying-geese unit to the right end of each unit. Make three, one *each* of red, pink, and navy (*fig. 2*).

3. Arrange the I rectangles and the step 2 units in a row as shown, noting the orientation of the middle unit. Join the pieces. Sew the J rectangles to opposite sides of the row (*fig. 3*).

Fig. 1

Make 1 of each unit,
1" × 1½".

Fig. 2

Make 1 of each unit,
1½" × 2½".

Fig. 3

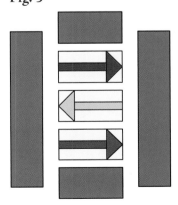

Whitestown

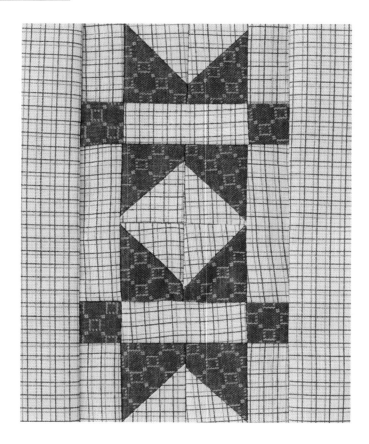

WHAT YOU'LL NEED

A: 8 light plaid squares, 1¼" × 1¼"

B: 4 light plaid rectangles, 1" × 1½"

C: 2 light plaid rectangles, 1" × 2"

D: 2 light plaid rectangles, 1" × 2½"

E: 2 light plaid rectangles, 1¼" × 5½"

F: 8 red rectangles, 1¼" × 1½"

G: 4 red squares, 1" × 1"

ASSEMBLY

Press the seam allowances open after sewing each seam unless directed otherwise.

1. Draw a diagonal line from corner to corner on the wrong side of each A square. Referring to "Stitch-and-Flip Corners" on page 192, join a marked A square to the upper-right corner of an F rectangle. Make four. Reversing the stitching direction as shown, repeat to make four reversed units (*fig. 1*).

2. Sew together two B rectangles and one of each unit from step 1. Make two (*fig. 2*).

3. Join a G square to each end of a C rectangle. Make two (*fig. 3*).

4. Arrange two of each unit from step 1 as shown. Sew the units together into two rows, and then join the rows. Sew the D rectangles to opposite sides of the unit (*fig. 4*).

5. Arrange the units from steps 2–4 in a row as shown. Join the units. Sew the E rectangles to opposite sides of the row (*fig. 5*).

Fig. 1

Make 4 of each unit, 1¼" × 1½".

Fig. 2

Make 2 units, 1½" × 3".

Fig. 3

Make 2 units, 1" × 3".

Fig. 4

Make 1 unit, 2½" × 3".

Fig. 5

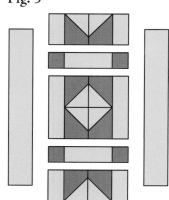

WHAT YOU'LL NEED

- **A:** 2 blue squares, 2" × 2"
- **B:** 2 blue rectangles, 1" × 4½"
- **C:** 1 blue rectangle, 1½" × 4½"
- **D:** 1 black rectangle, 2" × 3½"
- **E:** 3 red check squares, 1" × 1"
- **F:** 2 red check rectangles, 1" × 1¼"
- **G:** 2 light squares, 1" × 1"
- **H:** 2 light rectangles, ¾" × 1"
- **I:** 2 light rectangles, 1" × 1½"
- **J:** 1 light rectangle, 1" × 3"
- **K:** 2 light rectangles, ¾" × 2½"
- **L:** 1 light rectangle, 1" × 3½"
- **M:** 1 red rectangle, 1" × 1½"

ASSEMBLY

Press the seam allowances open after sewing each seam unless directed otherwise.

1. Draw a diagonal line from corner to corner on the wrong side of each A square. Referring to "Flying-Geese Units" on page 192, use the marked A squares and the D rectangle to make a flying-geese unit.

2. Sew together the E and G squares (*fig. 1*).

3. Lay out the F, H, I, and M rectangles as shown. Sew together the F and H rectangles in pairs, and then join the pieces in a row (*fig. 2*).

4. Sew together the J rectangle and the units from steps 2 and 3 as shown. Join the K rectangles to opposite sides of the unit (*fig. 3*).

5. Sew together the flying-geese unit, the L rectangle, and the step 4 unit as shown (*fig. 4*).

6. Sew the B rectangles to opposite sides of the step 5 unit and the C rectangle to the bottom (*fig. 5*).

Fig. 1

Make 1 unit,
1" × 3".

Fig. 2

Make 1 unit,
1½" × 3".

Fig. 3

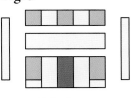

Make 1 unit,
2½" × 3½".

Fig. 4

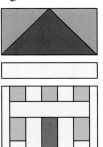

Make 1 unit,
3½" × 4½".

Fig. 5

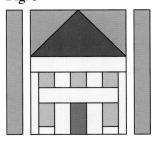

Stretch Dash

WHAT YOU'LL NEED

☐ **A:** 2 light squares, 2⅜" × 2⅜"; cut the squares in half diagonally to yield 4 triangles

☐ **B:** 2 light rectangles, 1¼" × 2½"

☐ **C:** 1 light rectangle, 1½" × 2½"

☐ **D:** 2 light rectangles, 1¼" × 1½"

■ **E:** 2 blue squares, 2⅜" × 2⅜"; cut the squares in half diagonally to yield 4 triangles

▨ **F:** 2 pink rectangles, 1¼" × 2½"

▨ **G:** 2 pink rectangles, 1¼" × 1½"

ASSEMBLY

Press the seam allowances open after sewing each seam unless directed otherwise.

1. Referring to "Half-Square-Triangle Units" on page 192, sew the A and E triangles together in pairs to make four half-square-triangle units measuring 2" square. Press the seam allowances toward the E triangles.

2. Sew together a B rectangle and an F rectangle. Make two (*fig. 1*).

3. Sew together a D rectangle and a G rectangle. Make two (*fig. 2*).

4. Arrange the half-square-triangle units, the units from steps 2 and 3, and the C rectangle as shown. Sew the pieces together into three rows, and then join the rows (*fig. 3*).

Fig. 1

Make 2 units, 2" × 2½".

Fig. 2

Make 2 units, 1½" × 2".

Fig. 3

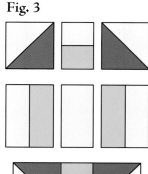

WHAT YOU'LL NEED

☐ **A:** 6 light squares, 1⅞" × 1⅞"; cut the squares in half diagonally to yield 12 triangles (you'll have 1 left over)

☐ **B:** 1 light square, 1½" × 1½"

☐ **C:** 2 light squares, 1" × 1"

■ **D:** 6 red squares, 1⅞" × 1⅞"; cut the squares in half diagonally to yield 12 triangles (you'll have 1 left over)

■ **E:** 4 red squares, 1½" × 1½"

■ **F:** 2 red rectangles, 1" × 4½"

ASSEMBLY

Press the seam allowances open after sewing each seam unless directed otherwise.

1. Referring to "Half-Square-Triangle Units" on page 192, sew the A and D triangles together in pairs to make 11 half-square-triangle units measuring 1½" square. Press the seam allowances toward the D triangles.

2. Draw a diagonal line from corner to corner on the wrong side of each C square. Referring to "Stitch-and-Flip Corners" on page 192, join a marked C square to one corner of an E square. Make two (*fig. 1*).

3. Arrange the remaining E squares, the half-square-triangle units, the B square, and the step 2 units as shown. Sew the pieces together into four rows, and then join the rows (*fig. 2*).

4. Sew the F rectangles to the top and bottom of the step 3 unit (*fig. 3*).

Fig. 1

Make 2 units,
1½" × 1½".

Fig. 2

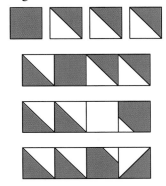

Make 1 unit,
4½" × 4½".

Fig. 3

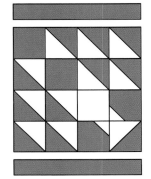

Jailbird

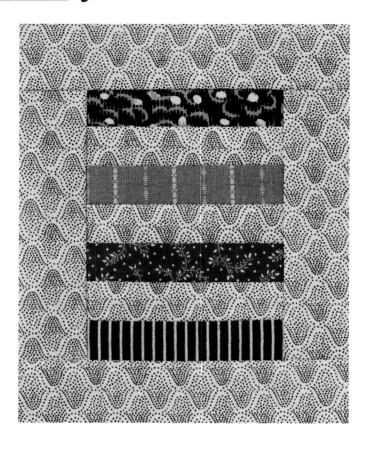

WHAT YOU'LL NEED

- **A:** 4 assorted blue rectangles, 1" × 3"
- **B:** 3 light rectangles, 1" × 3"
- **C:** 2 light rectangles, 1¼" × 4"
- **D:** 2 light rectangles, 1¼" × 4½"

ASSEMBLY

Press the seam allowances open after sewing each seam unless directed otherwise.

1. Sew together the A and B rectangles, alternating blue and gray (*fig. 1*).

2. Sew the C rectangles to opposite sides of the step 1 unit. Join the D rectangles to the top and bottom of the unit (*fig. 2*).

Fig. 1

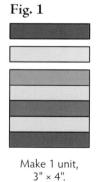

Make 1 unit,
3" × 4".

Fig. 2

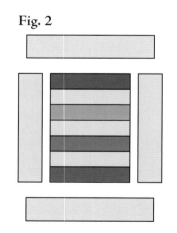

WHAT YOU'LL NEED

A: 16 assorted dark squares, 2½" × 2½"
(4 *each* of assorted black, pink, navy, and red
prints); cut the squares into quarters diagonally
to yield 64 triangles (you'll have 48 left over)*

B: 4 assorted dark squares, 2¾" × 2¾"
(1 *each* of black, pink, navy, and red prints
that are different from the A squares); cut the
squares into quarters diagonally to yield 16
triangles (you'll have 12 left over)

☐ **C:** 2 light rectangles, 1¾" × 2"

☐ **D:** 6 light rectangles, 1" × 1¾"

☐ **E:** 2 light rectangles, 1" × 4½"

*For a less scrappy block and no extra A triangles, cut 1 red,
1 black, 1 pink, and 1 navy A square, 2½" × 2½"; cut the
squares into quarters diagonally to yield 16 triangles.*

ASSEMBLY

Press the seam allowances open after sewing each seam
unless directed otherwise.

1. Join 16 of the A triangles in black/pink and navy/red
   pairs, using different prints for each pair. Make four
   of each (*fig. 1*).

2. Sew together one of each pair from step 1 to make
   a small quarter-square-triangle unit measuring 1¾"
   square. Make four (*fig. 2*).

3. Join four of the B triangles in black/pink and navy/
   red pairs, using one triangle from each print. Sew the
   pairs together to make a large quarter-square-triangle
   unit measuring 2" square. Sew the C rectangles to
   opposite sides of the unit (*fig. 3*).

4. Sew together three D rectangles and two small
   quarter-square-triangle units. Make two (*fig. 4*).

5. Arrange the E rectangles and the units from steps
   3 and 4 in five rows as shown (*fig. 5*). Sew the rows
   together.

Fig. 1

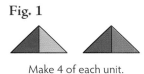

Make 4 of each unit.

Fig. 2

Make 4 units,
1¾" × 1¾".

Fig. 3

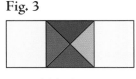

Make 1 unit,
2" × 4½".

Fig. 4

Make 2 units,
1¾" × 4½".

Fig. 5

Turn Signal

WHAT YOU'LL NEED

- **A:** 4 pink squares, 1" × 1"
- **B:** 4 pink rectangles, 1½" × 2½"
- **C:** 1 red square, 1½" × 1½"
- **D:** 2 light rectangles, 1" × 1½"
- **E:** 8 light squares, 1½" × 1½"
- **F:** 2 light rectangles, 1½" × 5½"

ASSEMBLY

Press the seam allowances open after sewing each seam unless directed otherwise.

1. Draw a diagonal line from corner to corner on the wrong side of each A square. Referring to "Stitch-and-Flip Corners" on page 192, join a marked A square to each corner of the C square (*fig. 1*).
2. Join the D rectangles to opposite sides of the step 1 unit (*fig. 2*).
3. Draw a diagonal line from corner to corner on the wrong side of each E square. Referring to "Flying-Geese Units" on page 192, use the marked E squares and the B rectangles to make four flying-geese units.
4. Arrange the step 2 unit and the flying-geese units in a row as shown. Join the units. Sew the F rectangles to opposite sides of the row (*fig. 3*).

Fig. 1

Fig. 2

Make 1 unit,
1½" × 2½".

Fig. 3

Make 1 unit,
1½" × 1½".

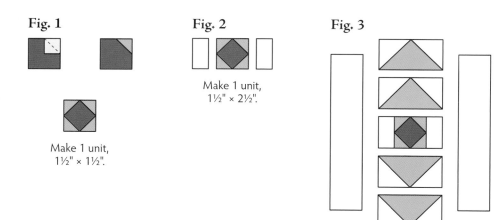

WHAT YOU'LL NEED

A: 4 blue squares, 2" × 2"

B: 2 navy rectangles, 1½" × 2"

C: 1 navy rectangle, 1½" × 4½"

D: 4 light rectangles, 2" × 2½"

E: 2 light rectangles, 1" × 1½"

ASSEMBLY

Press the seam allowances open after sewing each seam unless directed otherwise.

1. Draw a diagonal line from corner to corner on the wrong side of each A square. Referring to "Stitch-and-Flip Corners" on page 192, join a marked A square to the lower-right corner of a D rectangle. Make two. Reversing the stitching direction as shown, repeat to make two reversed units (*fig. 1*).

2. Sew together an E rectangle and a B rectangle. Make two (*fig. 2*).

3. Arrange the units from steps 1 and 2 and the C rectangle in three rows as shown. Sew together the units in the top and bottom rows, and then join the rows (*fig. 3*).

Fig. 1

Make 2 of each unit,
2" × 2½".

Fig. 2

Make 2 units,
1½" × 2½".

Fig. 3

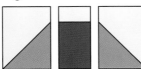

WHAT YOU'LL NEED

A: 6 red plaid squares, 1⅜" × 1⅜"; cut the squares in half diagonally to yield 12 triangles

B: 4 red plaid rectangles, 1" × 2"

C: 4 red plaid rectangles, ¾" × 1"

D: 2 red plaid rectangles, 1" × 1½"

E: 4 red plaid squares, 1" × 1"

F: 6 blue squares, 1⅜" × 1⅜"; cut the squares in half diagonally to yield 12 triangles

G: 1 blue square, 1" × 1"

H: 2 blue rectangles, ¾" × 3½"

I: 2 blue rectangles, ¾" × 4"

J: 4 light rectangles, 1" × 4½"

ASSEMBLY

Press the seam allowances open after sewing each seam unless directed otherwise.

1. Referring to "Half-Square-Triangle Units" on page 192, sew the A and F triangles together in pairs to make 12 half-square-triangle units measuring 1" square. Press the seam allowances toward the F triangles.

2. Sew a half-square-triangle unit to each end of a B rectangle. Make two (*fig. 1*).

3. Sew together two C rectangles, two half-square-triangle units, and a D rectangle as shown. Trim the seam allowances to ⅛". Make two (*fig. 2*).

4. Arrange four half-square-triangle units and the E and G squares as shown. Sew the pieces together into three rows, and then join the rows (*fig. 3*).

5. Sew B rectangles to opposite sides of the step 4 unit.

6. Arrange the units from steps 2, 3, and 5 as shown (*fig. 4*). Join the units.

7. Sew the I rectangles to opposite sides of the step 6 unit. Join the H rectangles to the top and bottom of the unit.

8. Sew J rectangles to opposite sides of the step 7 unit. Join the remaining J rectangles to the top and bottom of the unit (*fig. 5*).

Fig. 1

Make 2 units,
1" × 3".

Fig. 2

Make 2 units,
1" × 3".

Fig. 3

Make 1 unit,
2" × 2".

Fig. 4

Make 1 unit,
3" × 4".

Fig. 5

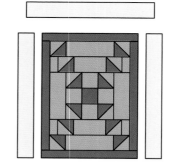

WHAT YOU'LL NEED

☐ **A:** 2 light rectangles, 1½" × 2½"

■ **B:** 3 burgundy rectangles, 1½" × 2½"

■ **C:** 2 burgundy rectangles, 1½" × 5½"

ASSEMBLY

Press the seam allowances open after sewing each seam unless directed otherwise.

1. Sew together the B and A rectangles (*fig. 1*).

2. Sew the C rectangles to opposite sides of the step 1 unit (*fig. 2*).

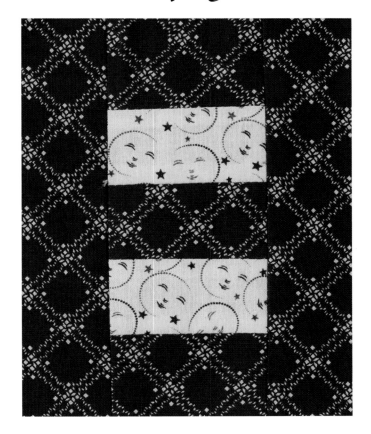

Fig. 1

Make 1 unit,
2½" × 5½".

Fig. 2

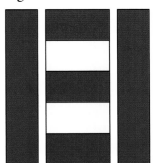

Simplicity

WHAT YOU'LL NEED

A: 2 light rectangles, 1½" × 3½"
B: 2 light rectangles, 1½" × 4½"
C: 1 blue rectangle, 2½" × 3½"

ASSEMBLY

Press the seam allowances open after sewing each seam unless directed otherwise.

1. Sew the A rectangles to opposite sides of the C rectangle (*fig. 1*).
2. Sew the B rectangles to the top and bottom of the step 1 unit (*fig. 2*).

Fig. 1

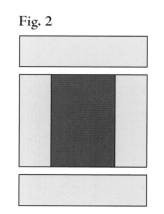

Make 1 unit,
3½" × 4½".

Fig. 2

WHAT YOU'LL NEED

A and B: 1 pink square, 8" × 8"

C and D: 1 black square, 8" × 8"

ASSEMBLY

Press the seam allowances open after sewing each seam unless directed otherwise.

1. Using the patterns on page 198, and referring to the patchwork and appliqué template instructions on page 192, cut two A pieces and two B pieces from the pink 8" square, and cut two C pieces and two D pieces from the black 8" square. Prepare the curved edges of the B and D pieces for your preferred appliqué method.

2. Referring to the photo for guidance, position the D pieces on the A triangles, and position the B pieces on the C triangles. Pin or baste the pieces in place.

3. Use your preferred appliqué method to sew the curved edges of the D and B pieces to the A and C triangles.

4. Sew the step 3 units together in pairs, and then join the pairs (*fig. 1*).

5. Carefully press the block with a pressing cloth, or turn the block over and press on the wrong side.

Fig. 1

Apple Seeds

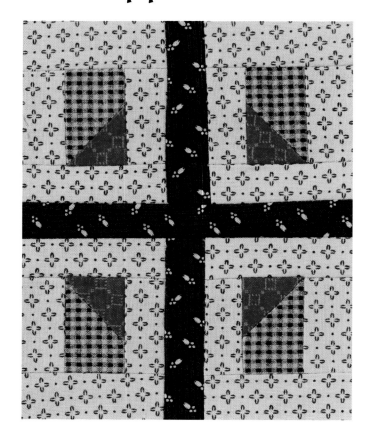

WHAT YOU'LL NEED

- **A:** 4 red squares, 1¼" × 1¼"
- **B:** 4 blue check rectangles, 1¼" × 1¾"
- **C:** 8 light rectangles, 1" × 1¾"
- **D:** 8 light rectangles, 1" × 2¼"
- **E:** 2 navy rectangles, 1" × 2¾"
- **F:** 1 navy rectangle, 1" × 4½"

ASSEMBLY

Press the seam allowances open after sewing each seam unless directed otherwise.

1. Draw a diagonal line from corner to corner on the wrong side of each A square. Referring to "Stitch-and-Flip Corners" on page 192, join a marked A square to the lower-right corner of a B rectangle. Make two. Reversing the stitching direction as shown, repeat to make two reversed units (*fig. 1*).

2. Sew C rectangles to opposite sides of a step 1 unit, and then join D rectangles to the top and bottom of the unit. Make two of each (*fig. 2*).

3. Arrange the step 2 units and the E and F rectangles in three rows as shown. Join the pieces in the top and bottom rows, and then sew the rows together (*fig. 3*).

Fig. 1

Fig. 2

Fig. 3

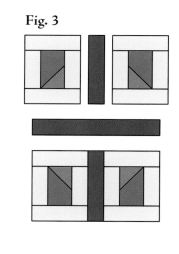

Make 2 of each unit,
1¼" × 1¾".

Make 2 of each unit,
2¼" × 2¾".

WHAT YOU'LL NEED

Positions 1–7: 7 blue scraps, about 1½" × 5" (1 of blue #1; 2 *each* of blue #2, #3, and #4)

A: 2 light rectangles, 1½" × 3½"

B: 2 light rectangles, 1½" × 2½"

C: 4 blue #3 squares, 1½" × 1½"

1 photocopy or tracing of the Diagonal Stripes paper-foundation piecing pattern below

ASSEMBLY

1. Using the prepared pattern and the assorted blue scraps, paper piece the block center. Refer to the photo and see the illustrated, downloadable Paper-Foundation Piecing tutorial at ShopMartingale.com/HowtoQuilt as needed.

2. Press the block center with a medium-hot iron, and then remove the foundation paper.

3. Arrange the block center, the A and B rectangles, and the C squares as shown. Sew the pieces together into three rows, and then join the rows (*fig. 1*). Press the seam allowances open.

Fig. 1

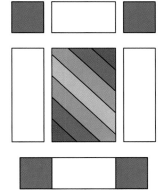

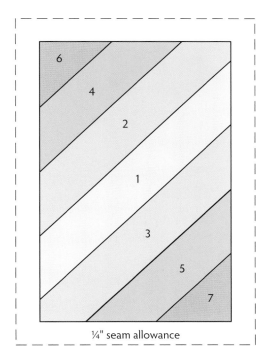

¼" seam allowance

WHAT YOU'LL NEED

☐ **A:** 8 light squares, 1" × 1"

■ **B:** 1 red rectangle, 2" × 2½"

■ **C:** 1 black rectangle, 2" × 2½"

■ **D:** 2 black #2 rectangles, 1½" × 2½"

■ **E:** 2 black #2 rectangles, 1½" × 5½"

ASSEMBLY

Press the seam allowances open after sewing each seam unless directed otherwise.

1. Draw a diagonal line from corner to corner on the wrong side of each A square. Referring to "Stitch-and-Flip Corners" on page 192, join a marked A square to each corner of the red B and black C rectangles. Make two (*fig. 1*).

2. Arrange the D rectangles and the step 1 units in a row as shown. Join the pieces. Sew the E rectangles to opposite sides of the row (*fig. 2*).

Fig. 1

Fig. 2

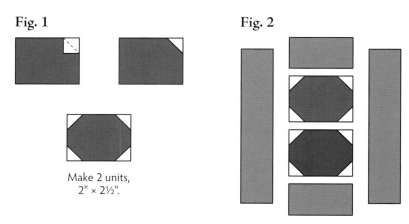

Make 2 units,
2" × 2½".

WHAT YOU'LL NEED

■ **Position 1:** 1 black scrap, about 2" × 2"

☐ **Positions 2 and 3:** 2 light scraps, about 2" × 3"

▨ **Position 4:** 1 red scrap, about 5" × 5"

☐ **Positions 5 and 6:** 2 light scraps, about 3" × 6"

1 photocopy or tracing of the Tree paper-foundation
   piecing pattern (page 199)

ASSEMBLY

1. Using the prepared pattern and the black, light, and red scraps, paper piece the block. Refer to the photo and the illustrated, downloadable Paper-Foundation Piecing tutorial at ShopMartingale.com/HowtoQuilt as needed.

2. Press the block with a medium-hot iron, and then remove the foundation paper.

Mainspring

WHAT YOU'LL NEED

- **A:** 4 red squares, 1⅞" × 1⅞"; cut the squares in half diagonally to yield 8 triangles
- **B:** 4 navy squares, 1⅞" × 1⅞"; cut the squares in half diagonally to yield 8 triangles
- **C:** 4 navy rectangles, 1" × 2½"
- **D:** 4 light rectangles, 1½" × 2½"

ASSEMBLY

Press the seam allowances open after sewing each seam unless directed otherwise.

1. Referring to "Half-Square-Triangle Units" on page 192, sew the A and B triangles together in pairs to make eight half-square-triangle units measuring 1½" square. Press the seam allowances toward the B triangles.

2. Sew together two half-square-triangle units. Make four (*fig. 1*).

3. Sew a C rectangle to the bottom of a step 2 unit. Join a D rectangle to the top of the same unit. Make two (*fig. 2*).

4. Position a step 2 unit as shown, and sew the unit to the left side of a D rectangle. Join a C rectangle to the top of the unit. Make two (*fig. 3*).

5. Arrange the units from steps 3 and 4 as shown. Sew the units together into two rows, and then join the rows (*fig. 4*).

Fig. 1

Make 4 units,
1½" × 2½".

Fig. 2

Make 2 units,
2½" × 3".

Fig. 3

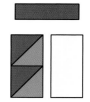

Make 2 units,
2½" × 3".

Fig. 4

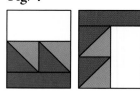
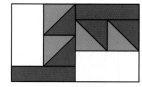

WHAT YOU'LL NEED

■ **A:** 4 red rectangles, 1½" × 2"

■ **B:** 1 red square, 1" × 1"

■ **C:** 4 red squares, 1¼" × 1¼"

□ **D:** 2 light plaid rectangles, 1" × 2"

□ **E:** 2 light plaid rectangles, 1" × 1½"

□ **F:** 2 light plaid rectangles, 1¼" × 3"

□ **G:** 2 light plaid rectangles, 1¼" × 4"

ASSEMBLY

Press the seam allowances open after sewing each seam unless directed otherwise.

1. Arrange the A, D, and E rectangles and the B square as shown (*fig. 1*). Sew the pieces together into three rows, and then join the rows.

2. Lay out the step 1 unit, the C squares, and the F and G rectangles as shown. Sew the pieces together into three rows, and then join the rows (*fig. 2*).

Fig. 1

Fig. 2

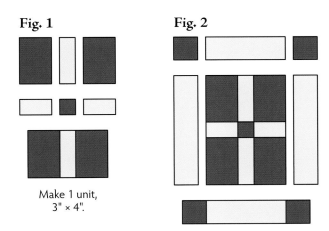

Make 1 unit,
3" × 4".

Shooting Star

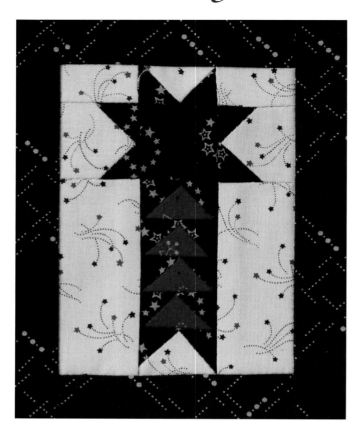

WHAT YOU'LL NEED

A: 16 blue #1 squares, 1" × 1"

B: 1 blue #1 square, 1½" × 1½"

C: 2 blue #2 rectangles, 1" × 3½"

D: 2 blue #2 rectangles, 1" × 5½"

E: 4 red rectangles, 1" × 1½"

F: 4 cream rectangles, 1" × 1½"

G: 2 cream squares, 1½" × 1½"

H: 2 cream rectangles, 1½" × 3"

ASSEMBLY

Press the seam allowances open after sewing each seam unless directed otherwise.

1. Draw a diagonal line from corner to corner on the wrong side of each A square. Referring to "Flying-Geese Units" on page 192, use eight marked A squares and four E rectangles to make four blue-and-red flying-geese units. Using four marked A squares and two F rectangles, repeat to make two blue-and-cream flying-geese units (*fig. 1*).

2. Sew an F rectangle to each end of a blue-and-cream flying-geese unit (*fig. 2*).

3. Referring to "Stitch-and-Flip Corners" on page 192, join A squares to both the upper-left and upper-right corners of a G square. Make two (*fig. 3*).

4. Sew the step 4 units to opposite sides of the B square (*fig. 4*).

5. Join four blue-and-red flying-geese units and one blue-and-cream flying-geese unit in a row as shown. Sew the H rectangles to opposite sides of the row (*fig. 5*).

6. Arrange the C rectangles and the units from steps 2, 4, and 5 in a row as shown. Join the pieces. Sew the D rectangles to opposite sides of the row (*fig. 6*).

Fig. 1

Make 4 units,
1" × 1½".   Make 2 units,
1" × 1½".

Fig. 4

Make 1 unit,
1½" × 3½".

Fig. 2

Make 1 unit,
1" × 3½".

Fig. 5

Make 1 unit,
3" × 3½".

Fig. 3

Make 2 units,
1½" × 1½".

Fig. 6

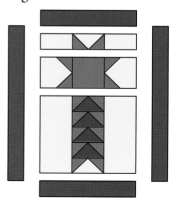

WHAT YOU'LL NEED

 A: 2 dark pink squares, 2¾" × 2¾"; cut the squares into quarters diagonally to yield 8 triangles

 B: 2 light pink squares, 2¾" × 2¾"; cut the squares into quarters diagonally to yield 8 triangles

C: 1 light pink square, 1½" × 1½"

D: 4 blue rectangles, 1½" × 2"

E: 2 light rectangles, 1" × 4½"

ASSEMBLY

Press the seam allowances open after sewing each seam unless directed otherwise.

1. Sew together two A triangles and two B triangles in pairs. Join the pairs to make a quarter-square-triangle unit measuring 2" square. Make four (*fig. 1*).

2. Arrange the quarter-square-triangle units, the D rectangles, and the C square as shown. Sew the pieces together into three rows, and then join the rows (*fig. 2*).

3. Sew the E rectangles to the top and bottom of the step 2 unit (*fig. 3*).

Fig. 1

Make 4 units,
2" × 2".

Fig. 2

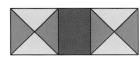

Make 1 unit,
4½" × 4½".

Fig. 3

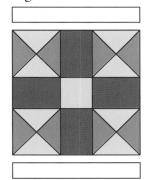

Good Luck

WHAT YOU'LL NEED

- **A:** 1 blue rectangle, 4" × 6"
- **B:** 2 blue rectangles, 2½" × 3"
- **C:** 1 light rectangle, 4" × 6"
- **D:** 2 light rectangles, 2½" × 3"

ASSEMBLY

Press the seam allowances open after sewing each seam unless directed otherwise.

1. Using the pattern below, and referring to the appliqué template instructions on page 192, cut two leaves from the A rectangle and two leaves from the C rectangle. Prepare the leaves for your preferred appliqué method.

2. Sew together the D and B rectangles in pairs, and then join the pairs (*fig. 1*).

3. Referring to the photo for guidance, position the leaves on the step 2 unit; place the A leaves on the D rectangles and the C leaves on the B rectangles. Pin or baste the pieces in place.

4. Use your preferred appliqué method to sew the leaf pieces in place. Carefully press the block with a pressing cloth, or turn the block over and press on the wrong side.

Fig. 1

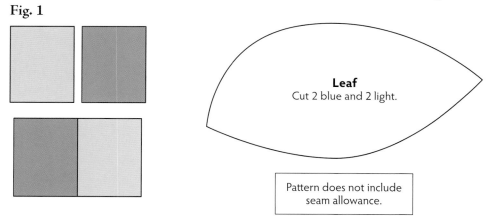

Leaf
Cut 2 blue and 2 light.

Pattern does not include seam allowance.

WHAT YOU'LL NEED

- **A:** 14 light squares, 1½" × 1½"
- **B:** 4 black rectangles, 1½" × 2½"
- **C:** 2 red rectangles, 1½" × 5½"

ASSEMBLY

Press the seam allowances open after sewing each seam unless directed otherwise.

1. Draw a diagonal line from corner to corner on the wrong side of 12 A squares.

2. Referring to "Stitch-and-Flip Corners" on page 192, join a marked A square to each end of a C rectangle as shown. Make two (*fig. 1*).

3. Use the stitch-and-flip technique to join a marked A square to each end of a B rectangle, paying attention to seam orientation. Make two.

4. Reversing the stitching directions as shown, repeat step 3 to make two reversed units (*fig. 2*).

5. Sew a step 3 unit to the left side of one of the remaining A squares, and join a step 4 unit to the right side of the square. Make two (*fig. 3*)

6. Arrange the units from steps 2 and 5 as shown (*fig. 4*). Join the units.

Fig. 1

Make 2 units,
1½" × 5½".

Fig. 2

Make 2 of each unit,
1½" × 2½".

Fig. 4

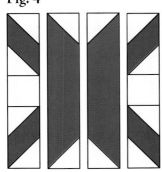

Fig. 3

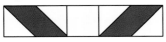

Make 2 units,
1½" × 5½".

Rook

WHAT YOU'LL NEED

■ **A:** 4 blue rectangles, 1" × 1½"
■ **B:** 5 blue squares, 1½" × 1½"
□ **C:** 2 light squares, 1½" × 1½"
□ **D:** 2 light rectangles, 1" × 1½"
□ **E:** 2 light rectangles, 1½" × 3½"
□ **F:** 2 light rectangles, 1½" × 2½"

ASSEMBLY

Press the seam allowances open after sewing each seam unless directed otherwise.

1. Arrange the A rectangles, the C squares, the D rectangles, and one B square as shown. Sew the pieces together into three rows, and then join the rows (*fig. 1*).

2. Lay out four B squares, the E and F rectangles, and the step 1 unit as shown. Sew the pieces together into three rows, and then join the rows (*fig. 2*).

Fig. 1

Fig. 2

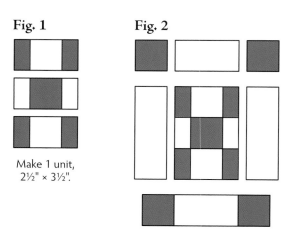

Make 1 unit,
2½" × 3½".

WHAT YOU'LL NEED

A: 4 rectangles, 1½" × 2" (1 *each* of pink #1, blue #1, pink #2, and blue #2)

B: 4 rectangles, 1½" × 2½" (1 *each* of pink #1, blue #1, pink #2, and blue #2)

C: 1 blue plaid rectangle, 2½" × 3½"

ASSEMBLY

Press the seam allowances open after sewing each seam unless directed otherwise.

1. Sew the A rectangles together in pairs, joining pink #1 to blue #1 and joining blue #2 to pink #2 (*fig. 1*).

2. Sew the B rectangles together in pairs, joining pink #1 to blue #2 and joining blue #1 to pink #2 (*fig. 2*).

3. Arrange the C rectangle and the units from steps 1 and 2 in three rows, matching the pink and blue prints as shown. Sew together the pieces in the middle row, and then join the rows (*fig. 3*).

Fig. 1

Make 1 of each unit, 1½" × 3½".

Fig. 2

Make 1 of each unit, 1½" × 4½".

Fig. 3

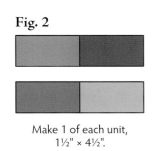

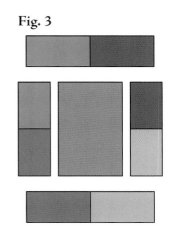

Cocktail

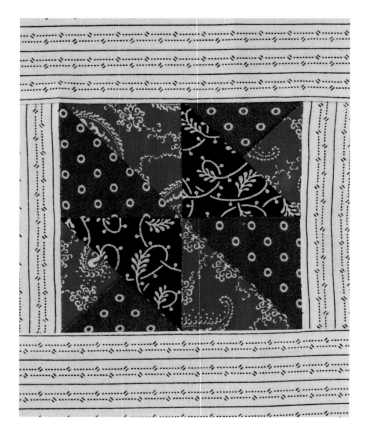

WHAT YOU'LL NEED

A: 1 red square, 2⅜" × 2⅜"; cut the square in half diagonally to yield 2 triangles

B: 1 red square, 2¾" × 2¾"; cut the square into quarters diagonally to yield 4 triangles (you'll have 2 left over)

C: 1 blue square, 2⅜" × 2⅜"; cut the square in half diagonally to yield 2 triangles

D: 1 blue square, 2¾" × 2¾"; cut the square into quarters diagonally to yield 4 triangles (you'll have 2 left over)

E: 1 black square, 2⅜" × 2⅜"; cut the square in half diagonally to yield 2 triangles

F: 2 light rectangles, 1" × 3½"

G: 2 light rectangles, 1½" × 4½"

ASSEMBLY

Press the seam allowances open after sewing each seam unless directed otherwise.

1. Referring to "Half-Square-Triangle Units" on page 192, sew the A and C triangles together in pairs to make two half-square-triangle units measuring 2" square. Press the seam allowances toward the C triangles.

2. Join a B triangle and a D triangle in a pair as shown. Sew an E triangle to the pair. Press the seam allowances toward the E triangle. Make two (*fig. 1*).

3. Arrange the half-square-triangle units and the step 2 units as shown. Sew the units together into two rows, and then join the rows (*fig. 2*).

4. Sew the F rectangles to opposite sides of the step 3 unit. Join the G rectangles to the top and bottom of the unit (*fig. 3*).

Fig. 1

Make 2 units,
2" × 2".

Fig. 2

Make 1 unit,
3½" × 3½".

Fig. 3

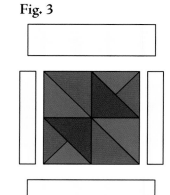

WHAT YOU'LL NEED

 A: 4 light squares, 1" × 1"

B: 4 light rectangles, 1¼" × 2"

C: 3 light rectangles, 1" × 1½"

D: 2 light rectangles, 1¼" × 4½"

E: 4 black squares, 1" × 1"

F: 4 red rectangles, 1½" × 2"

ASSEMBLY

Press the seam allowances open after sewing each seam unless directed otherwise.

1. Sew A squares to opposite sides of an E square. Make two (*fig. 1*).

2. Join two B rectangles, two F rectangles, and a step 1 unit as shown. Make two (*fig. 2*).

3. Sew together the C rectangles and two E squares, alternating them (*fig. 3*).

4. Arrange the D rectangles and the units from steps 2 and 3 as shown (*fig. 4*). Join the pieces.

Fig. 1

Make 2 units,
1" × 2".

Fig. 2

Make 2 units,
2" × 4½".

Fig. 3

Make 1 unit,
1" × 4½".

Fig. 4

WHAT YOU'LL NEED

☐ **A:** 6 light squares, 1⅝" × 1⅝"; cut the squares in half diagonally to yield 12 triangles

☐ **B:** 4 light squares, 1¼" × 1¼"

☐ **C:** 1 light square, 1½" × 1½"

☐ **D:** 2 light rectangles, 1" × 4½"

■ **E:** 6 red squares, 1⅝" × 1⅝"; cut the squares in half diagonally to yield 12 triangles

■ **F:** 4 blue rectangles, 1½" × 2"

ASSEMBLY

Press the seam allowances open after sewing each seam unless directed otherwise.

1. Referring to "Half-Square-Triangle Units" on page 192, sew the A and E triangles together in pairs to make 12 half-square-triangle units measuring 1¼" square. Press the seam allowances toward the E triangles.

2. Arrange three half-square-triangle units and a B square as shown. Sew the pieces together into two rows, and then join the rows. Make four (*fig. 1*).

3. Lay out the step 2 units, the F rectangles, and the C square as shown. Sew the pieces together into three rows, and then join the rows (*fig. 2*).

4. Sew the D rectangles to the top and bottom of the step 3 unit (*fig. 3*).

Fig. 1

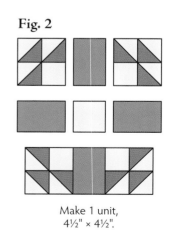

Make 4 units, 2" × 2".

Fig. 2

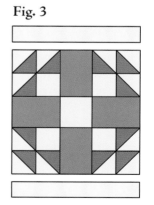

Make 1 unit, 4½" × 4½".

Fig. 3

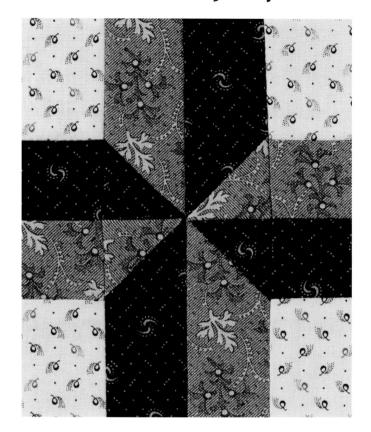

WHAT YOU'LL NEED

A: 4 light rectangles, 1½" × 2"

B: 2 blue rectangles, 1½" × 3"

C: 4 blue squares, 1½" × 1½"

D: 2 black rectangles, 1½" × 3"

E: 4 black squares, 1½" × 1½"

ASSEMBLY

Press the seam allowances open after sewing each seam unless directed otherwise.

1. Draw a diagonal line from corner to corner on the wrong side of two C squares and two E squares. Referring to "Stitch-and-Flip Corners" on page 192, join a marked E square to the lower-left corner of a B rectangle. Join a marked C square to the lower-right corner of a D rectangle. Make two of each (*fig. 1*).

2. Arrange the step 1 units as shown. Sew the pieces together into two rows, and then join the rows (*fig. 2*).

3. Sew together two A rectangles, one E square, and one C square. Make two (*fig. 3*).

4. Arrange the units from steps 2 and 3 as shown (*fig. 4*). Join the units.

Fig. 1

Make 2 of each unit, 1½" × 3".

Fig. 2

Make 1 unit, 2½" × 5½".

Fig. 3

Make 2 units, 1½" × 5½".

Fig. 4

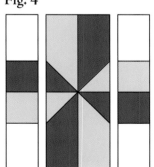

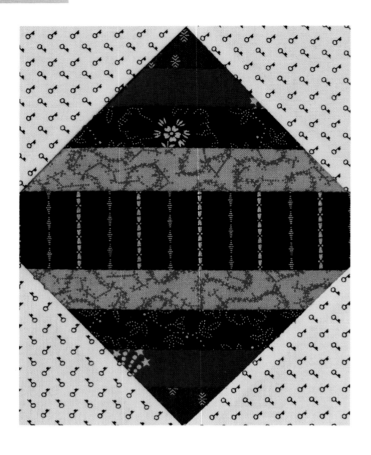

WHAT YOU'LL NEED

A: 4 strips, 1" × 9" (1 *each* of blue, red, black, and pink)

B: 1 navy rectangle, 1½" × 4½"

C: 4 light squares, 2½" × 2½"

ASSEMBLY

Press the seam allowances open after sewing each seam unless directed otherwise.

1. Join the A strips. Cut the unit in half as shown to make two segments measuring 2½" × 4½" (*fig. 1*).

2. Sew a step 1 segment to each long edge of the B rectangle (*fig. 2*).

3. Draw a diagonal line from corner to corner on the wrong side of each C square. Referring to "Stitch-and-Flip Corners" on page 192, join a marked C square to each corner of the step 2 unit (*fig. 3*).

Fig. 1

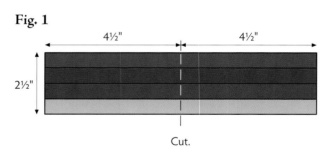

Cut.

Fig. 2

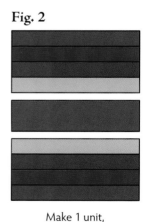

Make 1 unit,
4½" × 5½".

Fig. 3

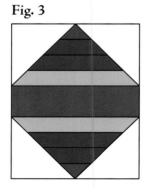

WHAT YOU'LL NEED

- **A:** 5 red squares, 1⅞" × 1⅞"; cut the squares in half diagonally to yield 10 triangles
- **B:** 5 light squares, 1⅞" × 1⅞"; cut the squares in half diagonally to yield 10 triangles
- **C:** 2 light rectangles, 1¼" × 5½"
- **D:** 2 black plaid rectangles, ¾" × 5½"

ASSEMBLY

Press the seam allowances open after sewing each seam unless directed otherwise.

1. Referring to "Half-Square-Triangle Units" on page 192, sew the A and B triangles together in pairs to make 10 half-square-triangle units measuring 1½" square. Press the seam allowances toward the A triangles.

2. Sew together five half-square-triangle units. Make two (*fig. 1*).

3. Arrange the C and D rectangles and the step 2 units as shown (*fig. 2*). Join the pieces.

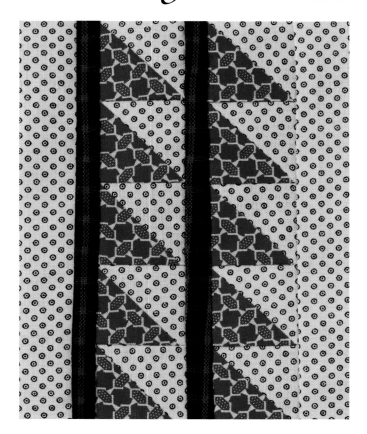

Fig. 1

Make 2 units, 1½" × 5½".

Fig. 2

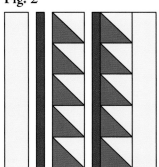

Snowball Nines

WHAT YOU'LL NEED

☐ **A:** 2 light rectangles, 2½" × 3"
☐ **B:** 8 light squares, 1¼" × 1¼"
■ **C:** 8 red squares, 1¼" × 1¼"
■ **D:** 2 red rectangles, 1" × 1½"
■ **E:** 4 blue rectangles, 1" × 1¼"
■ **F:** 4 blue rectangles, 1¼" × 1½"

ASSEMBLY

Press the seam allowances open after sewing each seam unless directed otherwise.

1. Draw a diagonal line from corner to corner on the wrong side of each C square. Referring to "Stitch-and-Flip Corners" on page 192, join a marked C square to each corner of an A rectangle. Make two (*fig. 1*).

2. Arrange four B squares, two E rectangles, two F rectangles, and one D rectangle as shown. Sew the pieces together into three rows. Join the rows. Make two (*fig. 2*).

3. Arrange the units from steps 1 and 2 as shown. Sew the units together into two rows, and then join the rows (*fig. 3*).

Fig. 1

Make 2 units,
2½" × 3".

Fig. 2

Make 2 units,
2½" × 3".

Fig. 3

WHAT YOU'LL NEED

- **A:** 9 dark blue check squares, 1⅝" × 1⅝"
- **B:** 6 light blue check squares, 1⅝" × 1⅝"
- **C:** 2 pink stripe rectangles, 1" × 4"
- **D:** 2 pink stripe rectangles, 1¼" × 4½"

1 paper or plastic template of a 3½" × 4" rectangle (page 197)

ASSEMBLY

Press the seam allowances open after sewing each seam unless directed otherwise.

1. Arrange the A and B squares in five rows as shown. Sew the pieces together into rows, and then join the rows (*fig. 1*).

2. Position the step 1 unit diagonally with right side up, and then place the 3½" × 4" rectangle template atop the unit (*fig. 2*; the dashed line indicates the seam allowance). Trace around the template and cut along the traced lines.

3. Sew the C rectangles to opposite sides of the step 2 unit. Join the D rectangles to the top and bottom of the unit (*fig. 3*). Note that the points of some squares will be slightly covered by the rectangles.

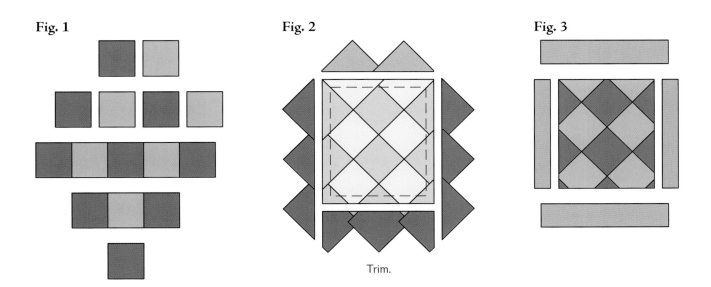

Fig. 1

Fig. 2

Trim.

Fig. 3

Pine Tree

WHAT YOU'LL NEED

☐ **A:** 2 light rectangles, 1½" × 2½"
☐ **B:** 2 light rectangles, 1½" × 2¼"
☐ **C:** 2 light rectangles, 1½" × 2"
☐ **D:** 2 light squares, 1½" × 1½"
☐ **E:** 2 light rectangles, 1½" × 2⅛"
☐ **F:** 1 blue #1 rectangle, 1½" × 2½"
☐ **G:** 1 blue #2 rectangle, 1½" × 3"
☐ **H:** 1 blue #3 rectangle, 1½" × 3½"
☐ **I:** 1 blue #4 rectangle, 1½" × 4½"
☐ **J:** 1 black rectangle, 1¼" × 1½"

ASSEMBLY

Press the seam allowances open after sewing each seam unless directed otherwise.

1. Place an A rectangle perpendicular to the left end of the F rectangle with right sides together. Sew diagonally across the corner of the A rectangle as shown, and then trim the seam allowances to ¼". Press the seam allowances toward A. In the same manner, stitch, trim, and press to add an A rectangle to the right end of the F rectangle (*fig. 1*).

2. Repeat step 1, sewing the B rectangles to the G rectangle, the C rectangles to the H rectangle, and the D squares to the I rectangle (*fig. 2*).

3. Sew the E rectangles to opposite ends of the J rectangle.

4. Arrange the units from steps 1–3 as shown (*fig. 3*). Join the units.

Fig. 1

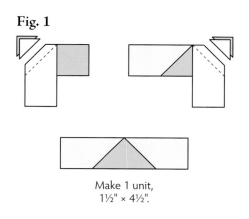

Make 1 unit,
1½" × 4½".

Fig. 2

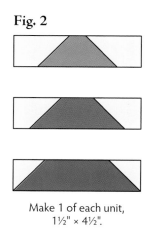

Make 1 of each unit,
1½" × 4½".

Fig. 3

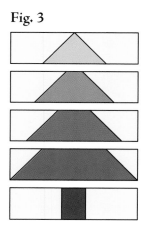

WHAT YOU'LL NEED

- **A:** 6 red #1 squares, 1⅞" × 1⅞"; cut the squares in half diagonally to yield 12 triangles
- **B:** 4 light squares, 1⅞" × 1⅞"; cut the squares in half diagonally to yield 8 triangles
- **C:** 2 red #2 squares, 1⅞" × 1⅞"; cut the squares in half diagonally to yield 4 triangles
- **D:** 4 red #2 squares, 1½" × 1½"
- **E:** 2 red #2 rectangles, 1" × 4½"

ASSEMBLY

Press the seam allowances open after sewing each seam unless directed otherwise.

1. Referring to "Half-Square-Triangle Units" on page 192, sew eight A triangles and the B triangles together in pairs to make eight half-square-triangle units measuring 1½" square. Press the seam allowances toward the A triangles. Sew the units together into four pairs (*fig. 1*).

2. Sew the remaining A triangles and the C triangles together in pairs to make four half-square-triangle units measuring 1½" square. Arrange the units as shown. Sew the units together into two rows, and then join the rows (*fig. 2*).

3. Lay out the D squares and the units from steps 1 and 2 as shown (*fig. 3*). Sew the pieces together into three rows, and then join the rows.

4. Sew the E rectangles to the top and bottom of the step 3 unit (*fig. 4*).

Fig. 1

Make 4 units,
1½" × 2½".

Fig. 2

Make 1 unit,
2½" × 2½".

Fig. 3

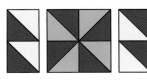

Make 1 unit,
4½" × 4½".

Fig. 4

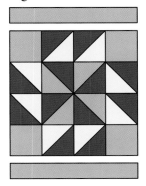

Fields

WHAT YOU'LL NEED

- **A:** 2 navy rectangles, $1\frac{1}{8}$" × 3"
- **B:** 2 navy rectangles, $1\frac{1}{4}$" × $2\frac{1}{2}$"
- **C:** 2 light rectangles, $1\frac{1}{4}$" × 3"
- **D:** 2 light rectangles, $1\frac{1}{2}$" × $2\frac{1}{2}$"
- **E:** 2 red rectangles, $1\frac{1}{8}$" × 3"
- **F:** 2 red rectangles, $1\frac{1}{4}$" × $2\frac{1}{2}$"

ASSEMBLY

Press the seam allowances open after sewing each seam unless directed otherwise.

1. Sew together A, C, and E rectangles. Make two (*fig. 1*).
2. Sew together B, D, and F rectangles. Make two (*fig. 2*).
3. Arrange the units from steps 1 and 2 as shown. Sew the units together into two rows, and then join the rows (*fig. 3*).

Fig. 1

Make 2 units, $2\frac{1}{2}$" × 3".

Fig. 2

Make 2 units, $2\frac{1}{2}$" × 3".

Fig. 3

WHAT YOU'LL NEED

A: 3 pink #1 squares, 1⅞" × 1⅞"; cut the squares in half diagonally to yield 6 triangles (you'll have 1 left over)

B: 5 pink #2 squares, 1⅞" × 1⅞"; cut the squares in half diagonally to yield 10 triangles (you'll have 1 left over)

C: 3 red squares, 1⅞" × 1⅞"; cut the squares in half diagonally to yield 6 triangles

D: 10 light squares, 1⅞" × 1⅞"; cut the squares in half diagonally to yield 20 triangles

ASSEMBLY

Press the seam allowances open after sewing each seam unless directed otherwise.

1. Referring to "Half-Square-Triangle Units" on page 192, sew A and D triangles together in pairs to make five half-square-triangle units measuring 1½" square. Repeat to make nine half-square-triangle units using B and D triangles, and make six half-square-triangle units using C and D triangles (*fig. 1*). Press all seam allowances toward the darker fabrics.

2. Arrange the half-square-triangle units as shown, noting the seam directions and fabric placement. Sew the units together into five rows, and then join the rows (*fig. 2*).

Fig. 1

Make 5 units,   Make 9 units,
1½" × 1½".   1½" × 1½".

Make 6 units,
1½" × 1½".

Fig. 2

Sail Away

WHAT YOU'LL NEED

▪ **A:** 1 black rectangle, 1" × 4½"

▪ **B:** 2 pink squares, 1½" × 1½"

▪ **C:** 2 pink squares, 2⅛" × 2⅛"; cut the squares in half diagonally to yield 4 triangles

▪ **D:** 2 pink rectangles, 1¼" × 3"

▪ **E:** 1 pink rectangle, 1" × 4½"

▪ **F:** 2 light squares, 2⅛" × 2⅛"; cut the squares in half diagonally to yield 4 triangles

▪ **G:** 1 blue rectangle, 1½" × 4½"

ASSEMBLY

Press the seam allowances open after sewing each seam unless directed otherwise.

1. Draw a diagonal line from corner to corner on the wrong side of each B square. Referring to "Stitch-and-Flip Corners" on page 192, join a marked B square to each end of the A rectangle (*fig. 1*).

2. Referring to "Half-Square-Triangle Units" on page 192, sew the C and F triangles together in pairs to make four half-square-triangle units measuring 1¾" square. Press the seam allowances toward the C triangles. Arrange the half-square-triangle units as shown. Sew the units together into two rows, and then join the rows (*fig. 2*).

3. Sew the D rectangles to opposite sides of the step 2 unit (*fig. 3*).

4. Arrange the E rectangle, the units from steps 1 and 3, and the G rectangle (*fig. 4*). Join the pieces.

Fig. 1

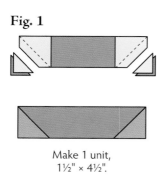

Make 1 unit,
1½" × 4½".

Fig. 2

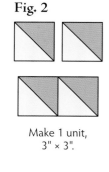

Make 1 unit,
3" × 3".

Fig. 3

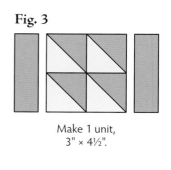

Make 1 unit,
3" × 4½".

Fig. 4

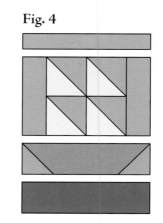

WHAT YOU'LL NEED

A: 6 navy rectangles, ¾" × 3½"

B: 2 navy rectangles, 1" × 3½"

C: 4 blue plaid rectangles, ¾" × 3½"

D: 1 blue plaid rectangle, 1" × 3½"

E: 4 light plaid rectangles, 1" × 4½"

ASSEMBLY

Press the seam allowances open after sewing each seam unless directed otherwise.

1. Sew together the A, C, and D rectangles as shown (*fig. 1*). Trim the seam allowances to ⅛".

2. Sew the B rectangles to the top and bottom of the step 1 unit (*fig. 2*).

3. Sew E rectangles to opposite sides of the step 2 unit. Join the remaining E rectangles to the top and bottom of the unit (*fig. 3*).

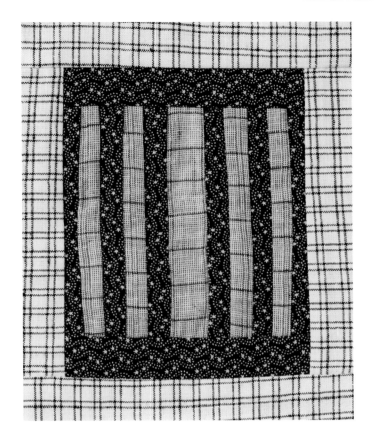

Fig. 1

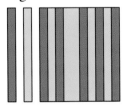

Make 1 unit,
3½" × 3½".

Fig. 2

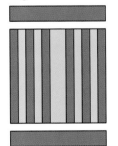

Make 1 unit,
3½" × 4½".

Fig. 3

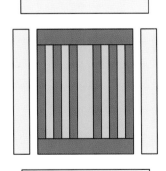

WHAT YOU'LL NEED

- **A:** 4 red rectangles, 1¼" × 1½"
- **B:** 1 red square, 1½" × 1½"
- **C:** 2 pink squares, 1½" × 1½"
- **D:** 2 pink rectangles, 1¼" × 1½"
- **E:** 2 light rectangles, 1½" × 3"
- **F:** 2 light rectangles, 1¼" × 5½"

ASSEMBLY

Press the seam allowances open after sewing each seam unless directed otherwise.

1. Arrange the A rectangles, the C squares, the D rectangles, and the B square as shown. Sew the pieces together into three rows, and then join the rows (*fig. 1*).

2. Sew the E rectangles to the top and bottom of the step 1 unit. Join the F rectangles to opposite sides of the unit (*fig. 2*).

Fig. 1

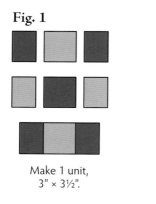

Make 1 unit,
3" × 3½".

Fig. 2

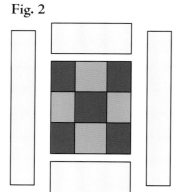

WHAT YOU'LL NEED

- **A:** 4 light squares, 1" × 1"
- **B:** 4 light squares, 1⅝" × 1⅝"; cut the squares in half diagonally to yield 8 triangles
- **C:** 2 light rectangles, 1¼" × 2½"
- **D:** 2 light rectangles, 1¼" × 1½"
- **E:** 2 light rectangles, 1¼" × 4"
- **F:** 2 light rectangles, 1¼" × 3"
- **G:** 2 blue rectangles, 1" × 1½"
- **H:** 4 blue squares, 1⅝" × 1⅝"; cut the squares in half diagonally to yield 8 triangles
- **I:** 1 blue square, 1½" × 1½"

ASSEMBLY

Press the seam allowances open after sewing each seam unless directed otherwise.

1. Draw a diagonal line from corner to corner on the wrong side of each A square. Referring to "Flying-Geese Units" on page 192, use the marked A squares and the G rectangles to make two flying-geese units. Sew the flying-geese units to the top and bottom of the I square (*fig. 1*).

2. Referring to "Half-Square-Triangle Units" on page 192, sew the B and H triangles together in pairs to make eight half-square-triangle units measuring 1¼" square. Press the seam allowances toward the H triangles.

3. Arrange four half-square-triangle units, the D and C rectangles, and the step 1 unit as shown. Sew the pieces together into three rows, and then join the rows (*fig. 2*).

4. Lay out four half-square-triangle units, the F and E rectangles, and the step 3 unit as shown. Sew the pieces together into three rows, and then join the rows (*fig. 3*).

Fig. 1

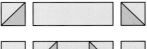

Make 1 unit,
1½" × 2½".

Fig. 2

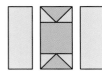

Make 1 unit,
3" × 4".

Fig. 3

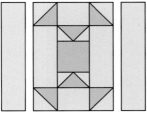

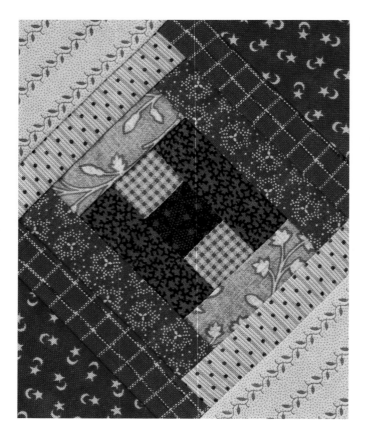

WHAT YOU'LL NEED

■ **Position 1:** 1 red #1 scrap, about 1½" × 1½"

■ **Positions 2 and 3:** 2 pink #1 scraps, about 1½" × 1½"

■ **Positions 4 and 5:** 2 red #2 scraps, about 1½" × 3"

■ **Positions 6 and 7:** 2 pink #2 scraps, about 1½" × 3"

■ **Positions 8 and 9:** 2 red #3 scraps, about 1½" × 4"

■ **Positions 10 and 11:** 2 pink #3 scraps, about 1½" × 4"

■ **Positions 12 and 13:** 2 red #4 scraps, about 1½" × 5"

■ **Positions 14 and 15:** 2 pink #4 scraps, about 2½" × 4"

■ **Positions 16 and 17:** 2 red #5 scraps, about 2½" × 4"

1 photocopy or tracing of the Stairwell paper-foundation piecing pattern (page 199)

ASSEMBLY

1. Using the prepared pattern and red and pink scraps, paper piece the block. Refer to the photo and the illustrated, downloadable Paper-Foundation Piecing tutorial at ShopMartingale.com/HowtoQuilt as needed.

2. Press the block with a medium-hot iron, and then remove the foundation paper.

WHAT YOU'LL NEED

■ **A and B:** 2 red plaid squares, 2⅜" × 2⅜" (one dark and one light); cut the squares in half diagonally to yield 4 triangles (you'll have 1 of each left over)

■ **C and D:** 2 blue plaid squares, 2⅜" × 2⅜" (one dark and one light); cut the squares in half diagonally to yield 4 triangles (you'll have 1 of each left over)

■ **E and F:** 2 pink plaid squares, 2⅜" × 2⅜" (one dark and one light); cut the squares in half diagonally to yield 4 triangles (you'll have 1 of each left over)

■ **G and H:** 2 black plaid squares, 2⅜" × 2⅜" (one dark and one light); cut the squares in half diagonally to yield 4 triangles (you'll have 1 of each left over)

□ **I:** 2 light rectangles, 1" × 3½"

□ **J:** 2 light rectangles, 1½" × 4½"

ASSEMBLY

Press the seam allowances open after sewing each seam unless directed otherwise.

1. Referring to "Half-Square-Triangle Units" on page 192, sew together one *each* of triangles A and B, C and D, E and F, and G and H in pairs to make four half-square-triangle units measuring 2" square (*fig. 1*). Press the seam allowances toward the darker triangles.

2. Arrange the half-square-triangle units as shown. Sew the units together into two rows, and then join the rows (*fig. 2*).

3. Sew the I rectangles to opposite sides of the step 2 unit. Join the J rectangles to the top and bottom of the unit (*fig. 3*).

Fig. 1

Make 1 of each unit, 2" × 2".

Fig. 2

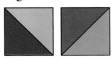

Make 1 unit, 3½" × 3½".

Fig. 3

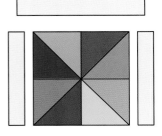

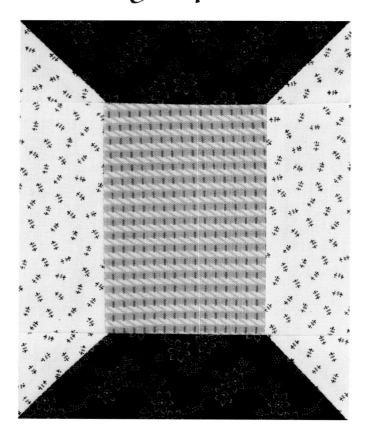

WHAT YOU'LL NEED

☐ **A:** 4 light squares, 1½" × 1½"

☐ **B:** 2 light rectangles, 1½" × 3½"

■ **C:** 2 black rectangles, 1½" × 4½"

▨ **D:** 1 pink rectangle, 2½" × 3½"

ASSEMBLY

Press the seam allowances open after sewing each seam unless directed otherwise.

1. Draw a diagonal line from corner to corner on the wrong side of each A square. Referring to "Stitch-and-Flip Corners" on page 192, join a marked A square to each end of a C rectangle. Make two (*fig. 1*).

2. Sew the B rectangles to opposite sides of the D rectangle (*fig. 2*).

3. Arrange the units from steps 1 and 2 as shown (*fig. 3*). Join the units.

Fig. 1

Make 2 units,
1½" × 4½".

Fig. 2

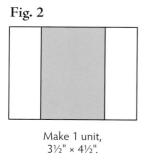

Make 1 unit,
3½" × 4½".

Fig. 3

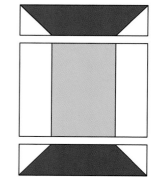

WHAT YOU'LL NEED

 A: 8 pink plaid squares, 1⅝" × 1⅝"; cut the squares in half diagonally to yield 16 triangles

B: 2 pink plaid squares, 1⅞" × 1⅞"; cut the squares in half diagonally to yield 4 triangles

C: 8 black plaid squares, 1⅝" × 1⅝"; cut the squares in half diagonally to yield 16 triangles

D: 2 black plaid squares, 1⅞" × 1⅞"; cut the squares in half diagonally to yield 4 triangles

E: 2 blue check rectangles, 1½" × 2"

F: 2 blue check rectangles, 1½" × 2½"

ASSEMBLY

Press the seam allowances open after sewing each seam unless directed otherwise.

1. Referring to "Half-Square-Triangle Units" on page 192, sew the A and C triangles together in pairs to make 16 small half-square-triangle units measuring 1¼" square. Press the seam allowances toward the C triangles.

2. Arrange four small half-square-triangle units as shown. Sew the units together into two rows, and then join the rows. Make four (*fig. 1*).

3. Sew the B and D triangles together in pairs to make four large half-square-triangle units measuring 1½" square. Sew the large half-square-triangle units together as in step 2.

4. Arrange the units from steps 2 and 3 and the E and F rectangles as shown. Sew the pieces together into three rows, and then join the rows (*fig. 2*).

Fig. 1

Make 4 units, 2" × 2".

Fig. 2

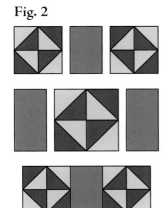

Bull's-Eye

WHAT YOU'LL NEED

- **A:** 1 blue plaid rectangle, 1½" × 2½"
- **B:** 2 black rectangles, 1¼" × 2½"
- **C:** 2 black rectangles, 1¼" × 3"
- **D:** 2 light stripe rectangles, 1¼" × 3"
- **E:** 2 light stripe rectangles, 1¼" × 5½"

ASSEMBLY

Press the seam allowances open after sewing each seam unless directed otherwise.

1. Sew the B rectangles to opposite sides of the A rectangle (*fig. 1*).
2. Join the C rectangles to the top and bottom of the step 1 unit (*fig. 2*).
3. Sew the D rectangles to the top and bottom of the step 2 unit. Join the E rectangles to opposite sides of the unit (*fig. 3*).

Fig. 1

Make 1 unit,
2½" × 3".

Fig. 2

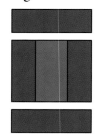

Make 1 unit,
3" × 4".

Fig. 3

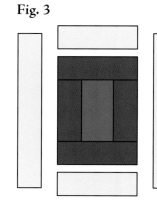

WHAT YOU'LL NEED

☐ **A:** 1 light strip, 1" × 32"
▨ **B:** 1 pink strip, 1" × 32"

ASSEMBLY

Press the seam allowances open after sewing each seam unless directed otherwise.

1. Join the A and B strips along the long edges to make a strip set. From the strip set, cut 20 segments measuring 1½" × 1½" (*fig. 1*).

2. Arrange the step 1 segments in five rows as shown. Sew the segments together into rows, and then join the rows (*fig. 2*).

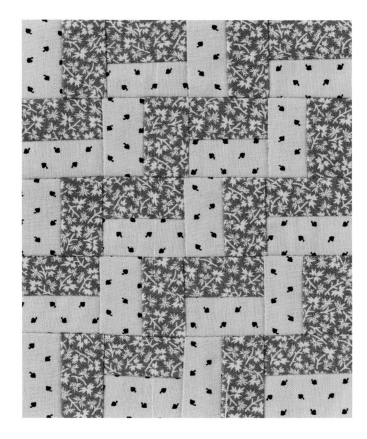

Fig. 1

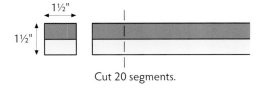

Cut 20 segments.

Fig. 2

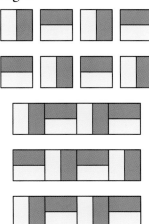

The Extra Mile

WHAT YOU'LL NEED

- **A:** 4 light rectangles, 1½" × 2"
- **B:** 8 red rectangles, 1" × 2"
- **C:** 1 red square, 1½" × 1½"
- **D:** 2 blue rectangles, 1½" × 2"
- **E:** 2 blue rectangles, 1½" × 2½"

ASSEMBLY

Press the seam allowances open after sewing each seam unless directed otherwise.

1. Sew together an A rectangle and a B rectangle. Make four (*fig. 1*).

2. Sew a B rectangle to the bottom of a step 1 unit. Make two. Rotate each remaining step 1 unit so that the B rectangle is on the left, and sew a B rectangle to the bottom of each of these units. Make two (*fig. 2*).

3. Arrange the step 2 units, the E and D rectangles, and the C square as shown. Sew the pieces together into three rows, and then join the rows (*fig. 3*).

Fig. 1

Make 4 units,
2" × 2".

Fig. 2

Make 2 of each unit,
2" × 2½".

Fig. 3

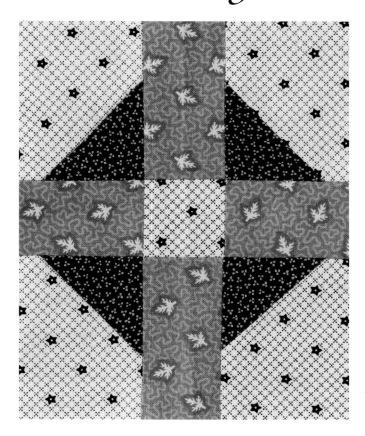

WHAT YOU'LL NEED

A: 4 light rectangles, 2" × 2½"

B: 1 light square, 1½" × 1½"

C: 4 blue squares, 1¾" × 1¾"

D: 2 pink rectangles, 1½" × 2½"

E: 2 pink rectangles, 1½" × 2"

ASSEMBLY

Press the seam allowances open after sewing each seam unless directed otherwise.

1. Draw a diagonal line from corner to corner on the wrong side of each C square. Referring to "Stitch-and-Flip Corners" on page 192, join a marked C square to the lower-right corner of an A rectangle. Make two. Reversing the square placement and stitching direction as shown, repeat to make two reversed units (*fig. 1*).

2. Arrange the units from step 1, the D and E rectangles, and the B square as shown. Sew the pieces together into three rows, and then join the rows (*fig. 2*).

Fig. 1

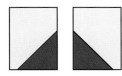

Make 2 of each unit,
2" × 2½".

Fig. 2

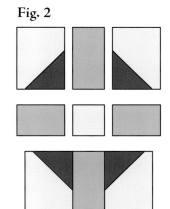

English Garden

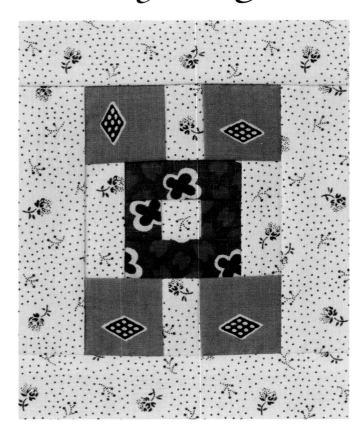

WHAT YOU'LL NEED

- **A:** 4 red squares, 1½" × 1½"
- **B:** 2 light rectangles, 1" × 1½"
- **C:** 1 light square, 1" × 1"
- **D:** 2 light rectangles, 1" × 2"
- **E:** 2 light rectangles, 1¼" × 4"
- **F:** 2 light rectangles, 1¼" × 4½"
- **G:** 2 blue squares, 1" × 1"
- **H:** 2 blue rectangles, 1" × 2"

ASSEMBLY

Press the seam allowances open after sewing each seam unless directed otherwise.

1. Join the G squares and the C square in a row as shown. Sew the H rectangles to the top and bottom of the row (*fig. 1*).

2. Arrange the A squares, the B and D rectangles, and the step 1 unit as shown. Sew the pieces together into three rows, and then join the rows (*fig. 2*).

3. Sew the E rectangles to opposite sides of the step 2 unit. Join the F rectangles to the top and bottom of the unit (*fig. 3*).

Fig. 1

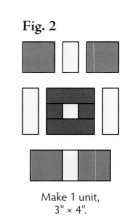

Make 1 unit, 2" × 2".

Fig. 2

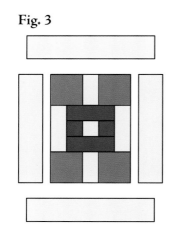

Make 1 unit, 3" × 4".

Fig. 3

WHAT YOU'LL NEED

☐ **A:** 3 light squares, 1⅞" × 1⅞"; cut the squares in half diagonally to yield 6 triangles (you'll use 5)

☐ **B:** 1 light square, 2⅞" × 2⅞"; cut the square in half diagonally to yield 2 triangles (you'll use 1)

☐ **C:** 2 light rectangles, ¾" × 3½"

☐ **D:** 2 light rectangles, 1" × 4"

■ **E:** 3 black squares, 1⅞" × 1⅞"; cut the squares in half diagonally to yield 6 triangles (you'll use 5)

■ **F:** 1 black square, 2⅞" × 2⅞"; cut the square in half diagonally to yield 2 triangles (you'll use 1)

■ **G:** 2 black rectangles, 1" × 4"

■ **H:** 2 black rectangles, ¾" × 5½"

ASSEMBLY

Press the seam allowances open after sewing each seam unless directed otherwise.

1. Referring to "Half-Square-Triangle Units" on page 192, sew the A and E triangles together in pairs to make five small half-square-triangle units measuring 1½" square. Press the seam allowances toward the E triangles.

2. Sew together a B triangle and an F triangle to make a large half-square-triangle unit measuring 2½" square. Press the seam allowances toward the F triangle.

3. Sew together two small half-square-triangle units. Join this unit to the right side of the large half-square-triangle unit (*fig. 1*).

4. Sew together three small half-square-triangle units. Join this unit to the top of the step 3 unit (*fig. 2*).

5. Sew the C rectangles to opposite sides of the step 4 unit. Trim the seam allowances to ⅛". Join the D rectangles to the top and bottom of the unit (*fig. 3*).

6. Sew the G rectangles to the top and bottom of the step 5 unit. Join the H rectangles to opposite sides of the unit (*fig. 4*). Trim the seam allowances to ⅛" to reduce bulk at the edge of the block.

Fig. 2

Make 1 unit,
3½" × 3½".

Fig. 4

Fig. 3

Make 1 unit,
4" × 4½".

Fig. 1

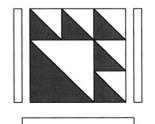

Make 1 unit,
2½" × 3½".

Snowball Fight

WHAT YOU'LL NEED

☐ **A:** 8 light rectangles, 1½" × 1¾"
■ **B:** 32 blue squares, ⅞" × ⅞"
☐ **C:** 8 pink dot rectangles, 1½" × 1¾"

ASSEMBLY

Press the seam allowances open after sewing each seam unless directed otherwise.

1. Draw a diagonal line from corner to corner on the wrong side of each B square. Referring to "Stitch-and-Flip Corners" on page 192, join a marked B square to each corner of an A rectangle. Make eight (*fig. 1*).

2. Arrange the step 1 units and the C rectangles as shown. Sew the pieces together into four rows, and then join the rows (*fig. 2*).

Fig. 1

Make 8 units,
1½" × 1¾".

Fig. 2

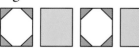

WHAT YOU'LL NEED

- **A:** 2 light #1 squares, 1⅞" × 1⅞"; cut the squares in half diagonally to yield 4 triangles
- **B:** 2 light #2 squares, 1⅞" × 1⅞"; cut the squares in half diagonally to yield 4 triangles
- **C:** 1 light #3 rectangle, 1½" × 2½"
- **D:** 1 light #4 rectangle, 1½" × 2½"
- **E:** 2 red squares, 1⅞" × 1⅞"; cut the squares in half diagonally to yield 4 triangles
- **F:** 2 blue squares, 1⅞" × 1⅞"; cut the squares in half diagonally to yield 4 triangles
- **G:** 4 navy rectangles, 1" × 4½"

ASSEMBLY

Press the seam allowances open after sewing each seam unless directed otherwise.

1. Referring to "Half-Square-Triangle Units" on page 192, sew the A and E triangles together in pairs to make four red half-square-triangle units measuring 1½" square. Press the seam allowances away from the light triangles. Using the B and F triangles, repeat to make four blue half-square-triangle units (*fig. 1*).

2. Arrange the red half-square-triangle units as shown. Sew the units together into two rows, and then join the rows to make a red pinwheel unit. Repeat with the blue half-square-triangle units to make a blue pinwheel unit (*fig. 2*).

3. Lay out the red and blue pinwheel units and the C and D rectangles as shown. Sew the pieces together into two rows, and then join the rows (*fig. 3*).

4. Sew G rectangles to opposite sides of the step 3 unit. Join the remaining G rectangles to the top and bottom of the unit (*fig. 4*).

Fig. 1

Make 4 of each unit, 1½" × 1½".

Fig. 2

Make 1 of each unit, 2½" × 2½".

Fig. 3

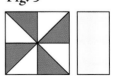

Make 1 unit, 3½" × 4½".

Fig. 4

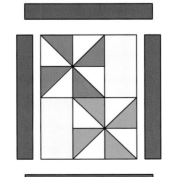

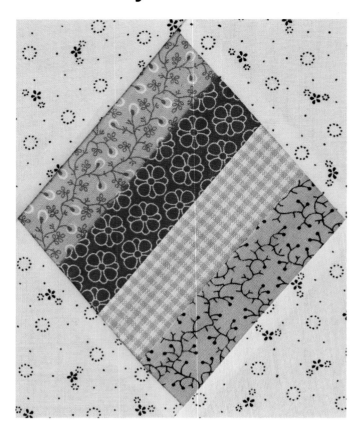

WHAT YOU'LL NEED

▢ **Positions 1–4:** 4 assorted pink scraps, about 1½" × 5" each

▢ **Positions 5–8:** 4 light scraps, about 3" × 5" each

1 photocopy or tracing of the Rafters paper-foundation piecing pattern (page 200)

ASSEMBLY

1. Using the prepared pattern and pink and light scraps, paper piece the block. Refer to the photo and the illustrated, downloadable Paper-Foundation Piecing tutorial at ShopMartingale.com/HowtoQuilt as needed.

2. Press the block with a medium-hot iron, and then remove the foundation paper.

WHAT YOU'LL NEED

- [ ] **A:** 1 light rectangle, 1½" × 4½"
- [ ] **B:** 2 light rectangles, 1½" × 1¾"
- [ ] **C:** 2 light squares, 1½" × 1½"
- [ ] **D:** 2 light rectangles, 1¼" × 1½"
- [ ] **E:** 2 light rectangles, 1" × 1½"
- [ ] **F:** 2 light squares, 1" × 1"
- [ ] **G:** 6 light squares, ¾" × ¾"
- [x] **H:** 1 red rectangle, 1½" × 2"
- [x] **I:** 1 red rectangle, 1½" × 2½"
- [x] **J:** 1 red rectangle, 1½" × 3"
- [x] **K:** 1 red rectangle, 1½" × 3½"

ASSEMBLY

Press the seam allowances open after sewing each seam unless directed otherwise.

1. Draw a diagonal line from corner to corner on the wrong side of each F square. Referring to "Stitch-and-Flip Corners" on page 192, join the marked F squares to both the upper-right and upper-left corners of the H rectangle. Sew the B rectangles to opposite ends of the unit (*fig. 1*).

2. Draw a diagonal line from corner to corner on the wrong side of each G square. Join a marked G square to each upper corner of the I rectangle as in step 1. Sew the C squares to opposite ends of the unit (*fig. 2*).

3. Join a marked G square to each upper corner of the J rectangle as in step 1. Sew the D rectangles to opposite ends of the unit (*fig. 3*).

4. Join a marked G square to each upper corner of the K rectangle as in step 1. Sew the E rectangles to opposite ends of the unit (*fig. 4*).

5. Arrange the A rectangle and the units from steps 1–4 as shown (*fig. 5*). Join the pieces.

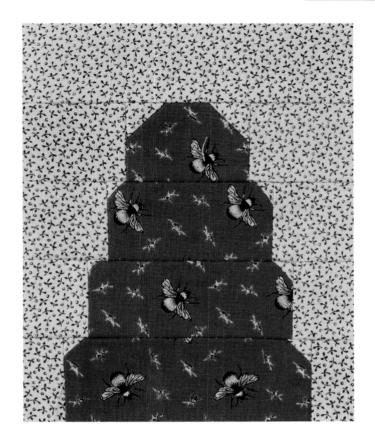

Fig. 2

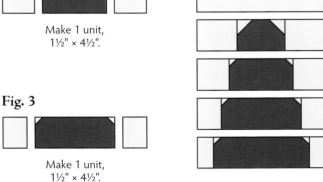

Make 1 unit, 1½" × 4½".

Fig. 3

Make 1 unit, 1½" × 4½".

Fig. 5

Fig. 1

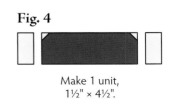

Make 1 unit, 1½" × 4½".

Fig. 4

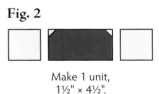

Make 1 unit, 1½" × 4½".

Friendship Star

WHAT YOU'LL NEED

☐ **A:** 2 light squares, 1⅞" × 1⅞"; cut the squares in half diagonally to yield 4 triangles

☐ **B:** 4 light squares, 1½" × 1½"

▨ **C:** 2 blue squares, 1⅞" × 1⅞"; cut the squares in half diagonally to yield 4 triangles

▨ **D:** 4 blue rectangles, 1" × 4½"

▨ **E:** 1 pink #1 square, 1½" × 1½"

▨ **F:** 2 pink #2 rectangles, 1" × 3½"

ASSEMBLY

Press the seam allowances open after sewing each seam unless directed otherwise.

1. Referring to "Half-Square-Triangle Units" on page 192, sew the A and C triangles together in pairs to make four half-square-triangle units measuring 1½" square. Press the seam allowances toward the C triangles.

2. Arrange the B squares, the half-square-triangle units, and the E square as shown. Sew the pieces together into three rows, and then join the rows (*fig. 1*).

3. Sew the F rectangles to the top and bottom of the step 2 unit (*fig. 2*).

4. Sew D rectangles to opposite sides of the step 3 unit. Join the remaining D rectangles to the top and bottom of the unit (*fig. 3*).

Fig. 1

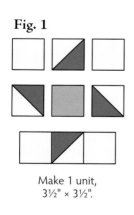

Make 1 unit,
3½" × 3½".

Fig. 2

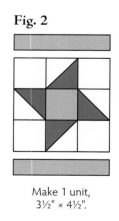

Make 1 unit,
3½" × 4½".

Fig. 3

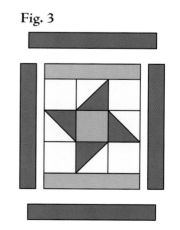

WHAT YOU'LL NEED

- **A:** 1 black #1 rectangle, 1" × 2"
- **B:** 4 black #1 squares, 1½" × 1½"
- **C:** 2 black #2 rectangles, 1¼" × 2"
- **D:** 2 black #2 rectangles, 1¼" × 2½"
- **E:** 2 pink dot rectangles, 1½" × 3½"
- **F:** 2 pink dot rectangles, 1½" × 2½"

ASSEMBLY

Press the seam allowances open after sewing each seam unless directed otherwise.

1. Sew the C rectangles to opposite sides of the A rectangle (*fig. 1*).

2. Join the D rectangles to the top and bottom of the step 1 unit (*fig. 2*).

3. Arrange the B squares, the F and E rectangles, and the step 2 unit as shown. Sew the pieces together into three rows, and then join the rows (*fig. 3*).

Fig. 1

Make 1 unit,
2" × 2½".

Fig. 2

Make 1 unit,
2½" × 3½".

Fig. 3

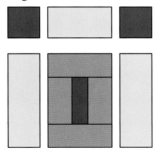

Apple Pie

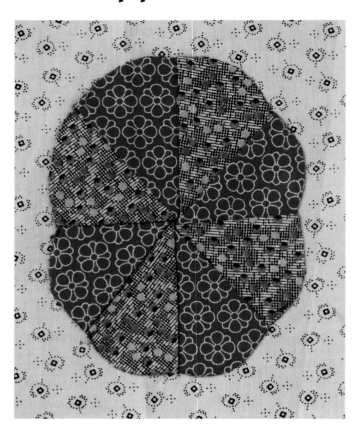

WHAT YOU'LL NEED

■ **A and C:** 1 red square, 6" × 6"
■ **B and D:** 1 blue square, 6" × 6"
□ **E:** 1 light rectangle, 5" × 6"

ASSEMBLY

1. Using the patterns below, and referring to the patchwork and appliqué template instructions on page 192, cut two A pieces and two C pieces from the red 6" square, and cut two B pieces and two D pieces from the blue 6" square.

2. Working clockwise, sew the step 1 pieces together in the following order: A, B, C, D, A, B, C, D (*fig. 1*). Lightly press all seam allowances in the same direction. Prepare the outer edges of the unit for your preferred appliqué method.

3. Center the step 2 unit on the E rectangle, and pin or baste it in place.

4. Use your preferred appliqué method to sew the step 2 unit to the E rectangle. Carefully press the block with a pressing cloth, or turn the block over and press on the wrong side. Trim the block to measure 4½" × 5½".

Fig. 1

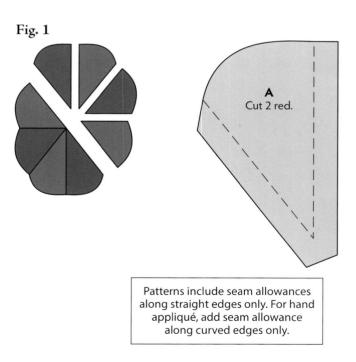

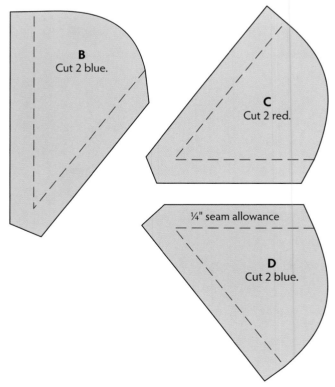

A
Cut 2 red.

B
Cut 2 blue.

C
Cut 2 red.

¼" seam allowance

D
Cut 2 blue.

Patterns include seam allowances along straight edges only. For hand appliqué, add seam allowance along curved edges only.

WHAT YOU'LL NEED

- **A:** 1 red square, 1½" × 1½"
- **B:** 2 pink #1 rectangles, 1" × 1½"
- **C:** 2 pink #2 rectangles, 1" × 2½"
- **D:** 2 pink #3 rectangles, 1" × 3½"
- **E:** 2 pink #4 rectangles, 1" × 4½"
- **F:** 2 blue #1 rectangles, 1" × 2½"
- **G:** 2 blue #2 rectangles, 1" × 3½"
- **H:** 2 blue #3 rectangles, 1" × 4½"

ASSEMBLY

Press the seam allowances open after sewing each seam unless directed otherwise.

1. Sew B rectangles to opposite sides of the A square (*fig. 1*).

2. Sew the F rectangles to opposite sides of the step 1 unit. Join the C rectangles to the top and bottom of the unit (*fig. 2*).

3. Sew the G rectangles to opposite sides of the step 2 unit. Join the D rectangles to the top and bottom of the unit (*fig. 3*).

4. Sew the H rectangles to opposite sides of the step 3 unit. Join the E rectangles to the top and bottom of the unit (*fig. 4*).

Fig. 1

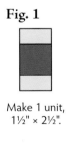

Make 1 unit, 1½" × 2½".

Fig. 2

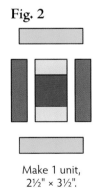

Make 1 unit, 2½" × 3½".

Fig. 3

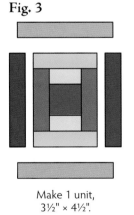

Make 1 unit, 3½" × 4½".

Fig. 4

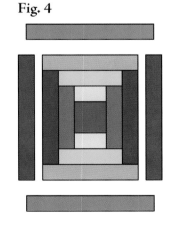

WHAT YOU'LL NEED

■ **A and C:** 1 red rectangle, 4" × 12"
▨ **B and D:** 1 blue rectangle, 4" × 12"
☐ **E:** 4 light rectangles, 1" × 4½"

ASSEMBLY

Press the seam allowances open after sewing each seam unless directed otherwise.

1. Using the patterns on page 200, and referring to the patchwork template instructions on page 192, cut eight small triangles (A) and two large triangles (C) from the red 4" × 12" rectangle. Cut eight small triangles (B) and two large triangles (D) from the blue 4" × 12" rectangle.

2. Layer an A triangle and a B triangle with right sides together. Place a pin through the intersections of the seam allowances to align the triangles properly. Sew the triangles together. Press the seam allowances toward the A triangles. Trim the unit to measure 1¼" × 1½". Make eight (*fig. 1*).

3. Arrange four step 2 units as shown. Sew the units together into two rows, and then join the rows. Make two (*fig. 2*).

4. Sew together a C and a D triangle as in step 2. Trim the unit to measure 2" × 2½". Make two.

5. Arrange the units from steps 3 and 4 as shown. Sew the units together into two rows, and then join the rows (*fig. 3*).

6. Sew E rectangles to opposite sides of the step 5 unit. Join the remaining E rectangles to the top and bottom of the unit (*fig. 4*).

Fig. 1

Make 8 units,
1¼" × 1½".

Fig. 2

Make 2 units,
2" × 2½".

Fig. 3

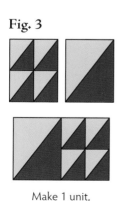

Make 1 unit,
3½" × 4½".

Fig. 4

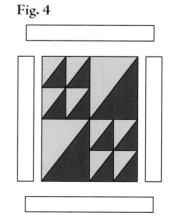

WHAT YOU'LL NEED

- **A:** 2 blue #1 squares, 1¼" × 1¼"
- **B:** 2 blue #2 rectangles, 1" × 1¼"
- **C:** 2 blue #2 rectangles, 1¼" × 1¾"
- **D:** 2 blue #3 rectangles, 1¾" × 2"
- **E:** 2 light rectangles, 1¼" × 3½"
- **F:** 2 light rectangles, 1½" × 4½"

ASSEMBLY

Press the seam allowances open after sewing each seam unless directed otherwise.

1. Sew together an A square and a B rectangle. Join a C rectangle to the top of the unit. Make two (*fig. 1*).

2. Arrange the D rectangles and the step 1 units as shown. Sew the pieces together into two rows, and then join the rows (*fig. 2*).

3. Sew the E rectangles to opposite sides of the step 2 unit. Join the F rectangles to the top and bottom of the unit (*fig. 3*).

Fig. 1

Make 2 units,
1¾" × 2".

Fig. 2

Make 1 unit,
3" × 3½".

Fig. 3

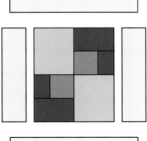

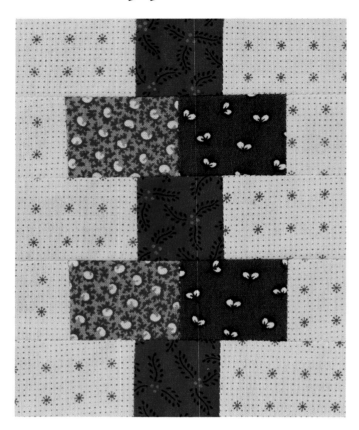

WHAT YOU'LL NEED

A: 6 light rectangles, 1½" × 2"

B: 4 light rectangles, 1¼" × 1½"

C: 3 red squares, 1½" × 1½"

D: 2 pink rectangles, 1½" × 1¾"

E: 2 blue rectangles, 1½" × 1¾"

ASSEMBLY

Press the seam allowances open after sewing each seam unless directed otherwise.

1. Sew A rectangles to opposite sides of a C square. Make three (*fig. 1*).

2. Sew together two B rectangles, one D rectangle, and one E rectangle as shown. Make two (*fig. 2*).

3. Arrange the units from steps 1 and 2 as shown (*fig. 3*). Join the units.

Fig. 1

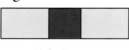

Make 3 units,
1½" × 4½".

Fig. 2

Make 2 units,
1½" × 4½".

Fig. 3

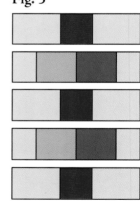

WHAT YOU'LL NEED

A: 20 black squares, 1" × 1"

B: 10 blue check squares, 1½" × 1½"

C: 20 blue check squares, 1" × 1"

ASSEMBLY

Press the seam allowances open after sewing each seam unless directed otherwise.

1. Arrange two A squares and two C squares as shown. Sew the squares together into two rows, and then join the rows. Make 10 (*fig. 1*).

2. Arrange the step 1 units and the B squares as shown. Sew the pieces together into five rows, and then join the rows (*fig. 2*).

Fig. 1

Make 10 units,
1½" × 1½".

Fig. 2

Crazy

WHAT YOU'LL NEED

Positions 1–9: 9 assorted blue, black, and red scraps, about 3½" × 3½"

A: 2 light rectangles, ¾" × 4½"

B: 2 light rectangles, 1" × 4½"

1 photocopy or tracing of the Crazy paper-foundation piecing pattern (page 201)

ASSEMBLY

1. Using the prepared pattern and the assorted blue, black, and red scraps, paper piece the block center. Refer to the photo and the illustrated, downloadable Paper-Foundation Piecing tutorial at ShopMartingale.com/HowtoQuilt as needed.

2. Press the block center with a medium-hot iron, and then remove the foundation paper.

3. Sew the A rectangles to opposite sides of the block center. Sew the B rectangles to the top and bottom of the unit (*fig. 1*). Press the seam allowances open.

Fig. 1

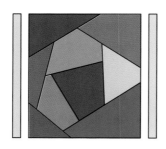

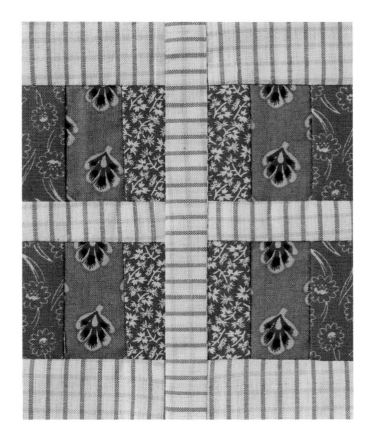

WHAT YOU'LL NEED

A: 4 pink #1 rectangles, 1" × 2"

B: 4 pink #2 rectangles, 1" × 2"

C: 4 blue rectangles, 1¼" × 2"

D: 2 light stripe rectangles, 1" × 2¼"

E: 4 light stripe rectangles, 1¼" × 2¼"

F: 1 light stripe rectangle, 1" × 5½"

ASSEMBLY

Press the seam allowances open after sewing each seam unless directed otherwise.

1. Sew together one A, one C, and one B rectangle. Make four (*fig. 1*).

2. Sew together two step 1 units, two E rectangles, and one D rectangle. Make two (*fig. 2*).

3. Arrange the step 2 units and the F rectangle as shown, noting the position of the pink #1 and pink #2 rectangles (*fig. 3*). Join the pieces.

Fig. 1

Make 4 units,
2" × 2¼".

Fig. 2

Make 2 units,
2¼" × 5½".

Fig. 3

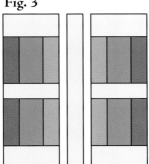

Argyle

WHAT YOU'LL NEED

A: 1 blue plaid rectangle, 5" × 8"

B: 1 light rectangle, 5" × 6"

ASSEMBLY

1. Using the pattern below, and referring to the appliqué template instructions on page 192, cut three diamond pieces from the A rectangle. Prepare the diamonds for your preferred appliqué method.

2. Referring to the photo for guidance, position the diamonds on the B rectangle. Pin or baste them in place.

3. Use your preferred appliqué method to sew each diamond to the B rectangle. Carefully press the block with a pressing cloth, or turn the block over and press on the wrong side. Trim the block to measure 4½" × 5½".

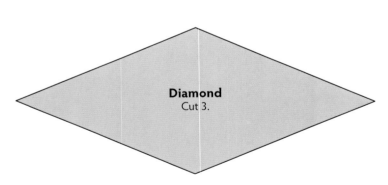

Diamond
Cut 3.

Pattern does not include
seam allowance.

WHAT YOU'LL NEED

☐ **A:** 7 light squares, 1⅞" × 1⅞"; cut the squares in half diagonally to yield 14 triangles

▨ **B:** 7 red squares, 1⅞" × 1⅞"; cut the squares in half diagonally to yield 14 triangles

▨ **C:** 1 black rectangle, 2½" × 3½"

ASSEMBLY

Press the seam allowances open after sewing each seam unless directed otherwise.

1. Referring to "Half-Square-Triangle Units" on page 192, sew the A and B triangles together in pairs to make 14 half-square-triangle units measuring 1½" square. Press the seam allowances toward the B triangles.

2. Sew together three half-square-triangle units, noting the color placement. Make two (*fig. 1*).

3. Sew together four half-square-triangle units, again noting the color placement. Make two (*fig. 2*).

4. Sew the step 2 units to opposite sides of the C rectangle, noting the color placement. Join the step 3 units to the top and bottom of the unit (*fig. 3*).

Fig. 1

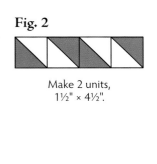

Make 2 units,
1½" × 3½".

Fig. 2

Make 2 units,
1½" × 4½".

Fig. 3

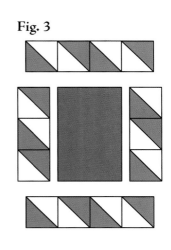

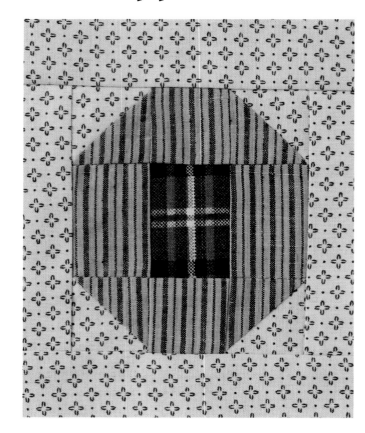

WHAT YOU'LL NEED

A: 2 blue stripe squares, 1⅞" × 1⅞"; cut the squares in half diagonally to yield 4 triangles

B: 2 blue stripe squares, 1½" × 1½"

C: 2 blue stripe rectangles, 1½" × 2"

D: 2 light squares, 1⅞" × 1⅞"; cut the squares in half diagonally to yield 4 triangles

E: 2 light rectangles, 1" × 4"

F: 2 light rectangles, 1¼" × 4½"

G: 1 blue plaid rectangle, 1½" × 2"

ASSEMBLY

Press the seam allowances open after sewing each seam unless directed otherwise.

1. Referring to "Half-Square-Triangle Units" on page 192, sew the A and D triangles together in pairs to make four half-square-triangle units measuring 1½" square. Press the seam allowances toward the A triangles.

2. Arrange the half-square-triangle units, the B squares, and the C and G rectangles as shown. Sew the pieces together into three rows, and then join the rows (*fig. 1*).

3. Sew the E rectangles to opposite sides of the step 2 unit. Join the F rectangles to the top and bottom of the unit (*fig. 2*).

Fig. 1

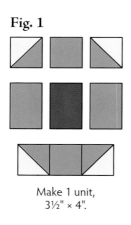

Make 1 unit, 3½" × 4".

Fig. 2

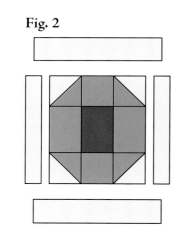

WHAT YOU'LL NEED

- **A:** 8 blue squares, 1¼" × 1¼"
- **B:** 7 pink squares, 1¼" × 1¼"
- **C:** 2 light rectangles, 1⅜" × 4¼"
- **D:** 2 light rectangles, 1⅛" × 4½"

ASSEMBLY

Press the seam allowances open after sewing each seam unless directed otherwise.

1. Arrange the A and B squares as shown. Sew the pieces together into three vertical rows, and then join the rows (*fig. 1*).

2. Sew the C rectangles to opposite sides of the step 1 unit. Join the D rectangles to the top and bottom of the unit (*fig. 2*).

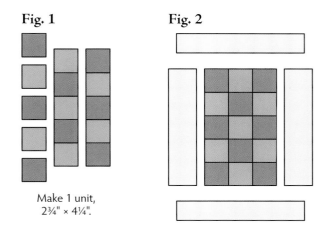

Fig. 1

Make 1 unit,
2¾" × 4¼".

Fig. 2

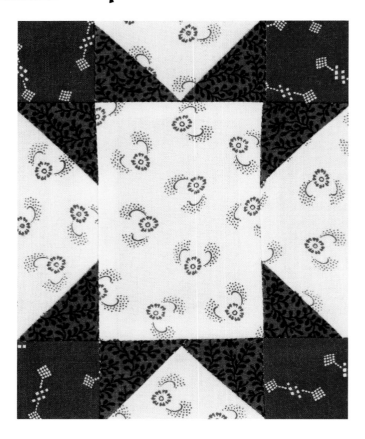

WHAT YOU'LL NEED

☐ **A:** 2 light rectangles, 1½" × 3½"
☐ **B:** 2 light rectangles, 1½" × 2½"
☐ **C:** 1 light rectangle, 2½" × 3½"
■ **D:** 8 red squares, 1½" × 1½"
■ **E:** 4 blue squares, 1½" × 1½"

ASSEMBLY

Press the seam allowances open after sewing each seam unless directed otherwise.

1. Draw a diagonal line from corner to corner on the wrong side of each D square.

2. Referring to "Stitch-and-Flip Corners" on page 192, join a marked D square to each end of an A rectangle. Make two (*fig. 1*).

3. Join a marked D square to each end of a B rectangle as in step 2. Make two (*fig. 2*).

4. Arrange the E squares, the units from steps 2 and 3, and the C rectangle as shown. Sew the pieces together into three rows, and then join the rows (*fig. 3*).

Fig. 1

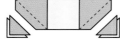 

Make 2 units,
1½" × 3½".

Fig. 2

Make 2 units,
1½" × 2½".

Fig. 3

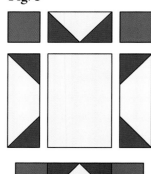

WHAT YOU'LL NEED

A: 1 black rectangle, 1½" × 2"

B: 2 red rectangles, 1" × 2"

C: 2 red rectangles, 1" × 2½"

D: 2 blue check rectangles, 1" × 3"

E: 2 blue check rectangles, 1" × 3½"

F: 2 light rectangles, 1" × 4"

G: 2 light rectangles, 1¼" × 4½"

ASSEMBLY

Press the seam allowances open after sewing each seam unless directed otherwise.

1. Sew the B rectangles to opposite sides of the A rectangle. Join the C rectangles to the top and bottom of the unit (*fig. 1*).

2. Sew the D rectangles to opposite sides of the step 1 unit. Join the E rectangles to the top and bottom of the unit (*fig. 2*).

3. Sew the F rectangles to opposite sides of the step 2 unit. Join the G rectangles to the top and bottom of the unit (*fig. 3*).

Fig. 1

Make 1 unit,
2½" × 3".

Fig. 2

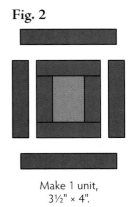

Make 1 unit,
3½" × 4".

Fig. 3

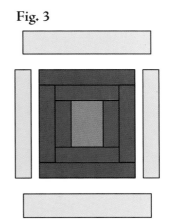

Mountain View

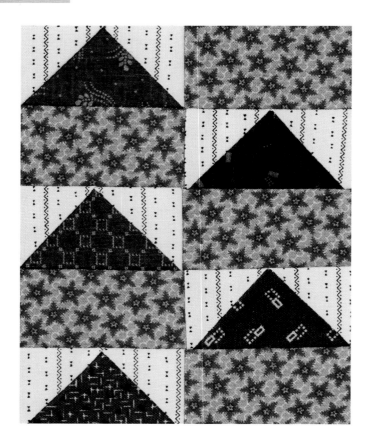

WHAT YOU'LL NEED

☐ **A:** 10 light squares, 1½" × 1½"
▨ **B:** 5 pink rectangles, 1½" × 2½"
■ **C:** 5 assorted blue rectangles, 1½" × 2½"

ASSEMBLY

Press the seam allowances open after sewing each seam unless directed otherwise.

1. Draw a diagonal line from corner to corner on the wrong side of each A square. Referring to "Flying-Geese Units" on page 192, use the marked A squares and the C rectangles to make five flying-geese units.

2. Arrange the flying-geese units and the B rectangles as shown. Sew the pieces together into five rows, and then join the rows (*fig. 1*).

Fig. 1

WHAT YOU'LL NEED

A: 1 blue #1 rectangle, 1½" × 3¼"

B: 1 blue #2 rectangle, 1¼" × 3¼"

C: 1 blue #3 rectangle, 1½" × 3¼"

D: 2 light squares, 3" × 3"; cut the squares in half diagonally to yield 4 triangles

E: 2 black rectangles, 1" × 4½"

ASSEMBLY

Press the seam allowances open after sewing each seam unless directed otherwise.

1. Sew together the A, B, and C rectangles as shown, with the narrower B rectangle in the center (*fig. 1*).

2. Sew D triangles to the top and bottom of the step 1 unit. Press the seam allowances toward the triangles. Join the remaining D triangles to opposite sides of the unit, and press as before (*fig. 2*).

3. Square up the step 2 unit to measure 4½" × 4½". Sew the E rectangles to the top and bottom of the unit (*fig. 3*).

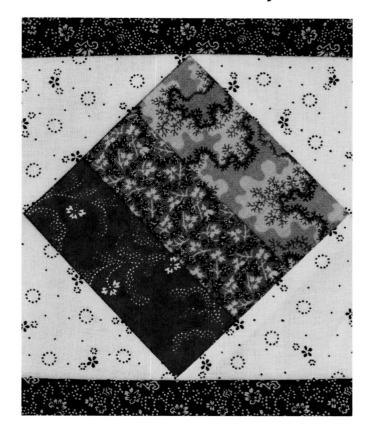

Fig. 1

Make 1 unit,
3¼" × 3¼".

Fig. 2

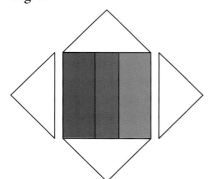

Fig. 3

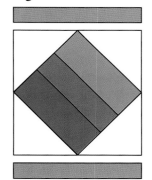

Aunt Nellie

WHAT YOU'LL NEED

- **A:** 2 light rectangles, 1" × 1½"
- **B:** 2 light rectangles, 1¼" × 1½"
- **C:** 2 light rectangles, 1" × 3"
- **D:** 2 light rectangles, 1¼" × 2½"
- **E:** 4 light rectangles, 1" × 4½"
- **F:** 1 red square, 1½" × 1½"
- **G:** 8 red rectangles, 1" × 1¼"

ASSEMBLY

Press the seam allowances open after sewing each seam unless directed otherwise.

1. Arrange four G rectangles, the B and A rectangles, and the F square as shown. Sew the pieces together into three rows, and then join the rows (*fig. 1*).

2. Lay out four G rectangles, the D and C rectangles, and the step 1 unit as shown. Sew the pieces together into three rows, and then join the rows (*fig. 2*).

3. Sew E rectangles to opposite sides of the step 2 unit. Join the remaining E rectangles to the top and bottom of the unit (*fig. 3*).

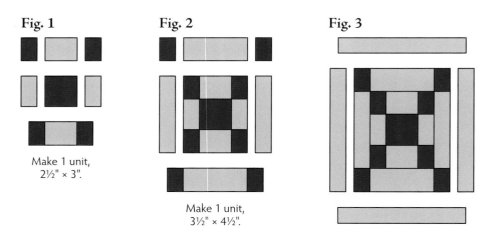

Fig. 1

Make 1 unit,
2½" × 3".

Fig. 2

Make 1 unit,
3½" × 4½".

Fig. 3

WHAT YOU'LL NEED

- **A:** 8 assorted black squares, 1¼" × 1¼"
  (2 *each* of 4 different prints)
- **B:** 4 blue stripe rectangles, 2½" × 3"
  (cut 2 with the stripes running horizontally
  and 2 with the stripes running vertically)

ASSEMBLY

Press the seam allowances open after sewing each seam unless directed otherwise.

1. Draw a diagonal line from corner to corner on the wrong side of each A square. Referring to "Stitch-and-Flip Corners" on page 192, join matching marked A squares to both the upper-left and lower-right corners of a B rectangle. Make four (*fig. 1*).

2. Arrange the step 1 units, alternating the stripe directions as shown in the photo. Sew the units together into two rows, and then join the rows (*fig. 2*).

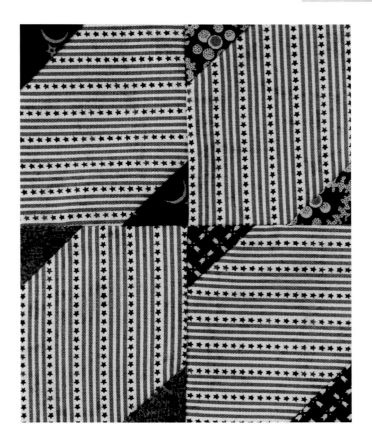

Fig. 1

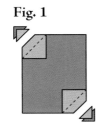

Make 4 units,
2½" × 3".

Fig. 2

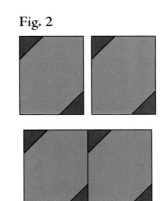

Steps

WHAT YOU'LL NEED

A: 4 blue rectangles, 1¼" × 2"
B: 1 pink rectangle, 1" × 1¼"
C: 2 pink rectangles, 1¼" × 2"
D: 2 black rectangles, 1" × 1¼"
E: 1 black rectangle, 1¼" × 1½"
F: 2 red rectangles, 1¼" × 2"
G: 1 red rectangle, 1¼" × 1½"
H: 1 red rectangle, 1" × 1¼"
I: 4 light rectangles, 1" × 4½"

ASSEMBLY

Press the seam allowances open after sewing each seam unless directed otherwise.

1. Arrange the A–H rectangles as shown. Sew the pieces together into four rows. Join the rows (*fig. 1*).

2. Sew I rectangles to opposite sides of the step 1 unit. Join the remaining I rectangles to the top and bottom of the unit (*fig. 2*).

Fig. 1

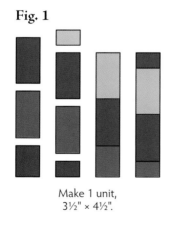

Make 1 unit,
3½" × 4½".

Fig. 2

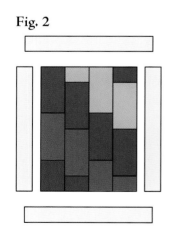

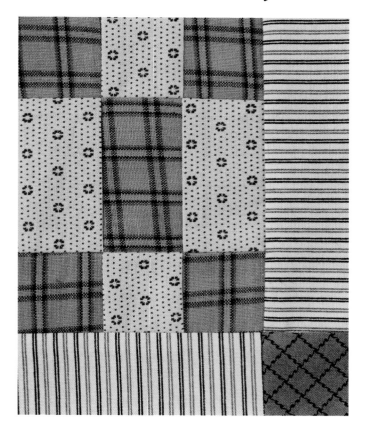

WHAT YOU'LL NEED

- **A:** 2 light #1 squares, 1½" × 1½"
- **B:** 2 light #1 rectangles, 1½" × 2½"
- **C:** 1 light #2 rectangle, 1½" × 4½"
- **D:** 1 light #2 rectangle, 1½" × 3½"
- **E:** 4 pink plaid squares, 1½" × 1½"
- **F:** 1 pink plaid rectangle, 1½" × 2½"
- **G:** 1 blue square, 1½" × 1½"

ASSEMBLY

Press the seam allowances open after sewing each seam unless directed otherwise.

1. Arrange the E and A squares and the B and F rectangles as shown. Sew the pieces together into three rows, and then join the rows (*fig. 1*).

2. Lay out the step 1 unit, the C and D rectangles, and the G square as shown. Sew the pieces together into two rows, and then join the rows (*fig. 2*).

Fig. 1

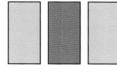

Make 1 unit,
3½" × 4½".

Fig. 2

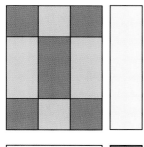

Old Maid

WHAT YOU'LL NEED

☐ **A:** 2 light squares, 2¾" × 2¾"; cut the squares into quarters diagonally to yield 8 triangles

■ **B:** 2 red squares, 2¾" × 2¾"; cut the squares into quarters diagonally to yield 8 triangles

■ **C:** 2 red rectangles, 1" × 4½"

■ **D:** 2 black rectangles, 1" × 3½"

■ **E:** 2 black rectangles, 1" × 4½"

ASSEMBLY

Press the seam allowances open after sewing each seam unless directed otherwise.

1. Sew together two A triangles and two B triangles in pairs. Join the pairs to make a quarter-square-triangle unit measuring 2" square. Make four (*fig. 1*).

2. Arrange the quarter-square-triangle units as shown. Sew the units together into two rows, and then join the rows (*fig. 2*).

3. Sew the D rectangles to the top and bottom of the step 2 unit. Join the E rectangles to opposite sides of the unit (*fig. 3*).

4. Sew the C rectangles to the top and bottom of the step 3 unit (*fig. 4*).

Fig. 1

Make 4 units,
2" × 2".

Fig. 3

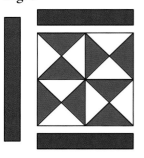

Make 1 unit,
4½" × 4½".

Fig. 4

Fig. 2

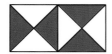

Make 1 unit,
3½" × 3½".

WHAT YOU'LL NEED

☐ **Position 1:** 1 light scrap, about 2" × 6"

■ **Positions 2 and 3:** 2 blue scraps, about 3" × 5"

■ **A:** 4 blue squares, 1¼" × 1¼"

☐ **B:** 2 light rectangles, 1¼" × 3"

☐ **C:** 2 light rectangles, 1¼" × 4"

1 photocopy or tracing of the Signature paper-foundation piecing pattern (page 201)

Fine-point permanent fabric marker

ASSEMBLY

1. Using the prepared pattern and the light and blue scraps, paper piece the block center. Refer to the photo and the illustrated, downloadable Paper-Foundation Piecing tutorial at ShopMartingale.com/HowtoQuilt as needed.

2. Press the block center with a medium-hot iron, and then remove the foundation paper.

3. Arrange the block center, the A squares, and the B and C rectangles as shown. Sew the pieces together into three rows, and then join the rows (*fig. 1*). Press the seam allowances open.

4. If desired, use a fine-point permanent fabric marker to add a signat ure to the light strip in the block center.

Fig. 1

Many of the blocks in this book use one or more of the following piecing methods. Refer to the individual block instructions for complete information about cutting the necessary pieces and marking squares, if necessary.

HALF-SQUARE-TRIANGLE UNITS

A half-square-triangle unit consists of two same-size triangles that have been created by cutting squares in half diagonally. Layer the triangles with right sides together and edges aligned. Join the triangles by stitching along the long diagonal edges using a ¼" seam allowance, and then flip the top triangle open. Press the seam allowances as directed in the block instructions (usually toward the darker triangle).

STITCH-AND-FLIP CORNERS

This stitch-and-flip technique is used to add a square to the corner of a larger piece, either another square or a rectangle. A smaller square may be added to only one corner or to each corner of the larger piece, depending on the block design. Start by marking the smaller square on the wrong side, as described in the block instructions. Then place the marked square on the desired corner of the larger square or rectangle with right sides together. Stitch along the drawn line, and then trim the seam allowances to ¼". Flip the resulting corner triangle open. Press the seam allowances toward the corner.

FLYING-GEESE UNITS

Each flying-geese unit begins with two marked squares, as described in the block instructions, and one rectangle. Place a marked square on the left end of the rectangle with right sides together. Stitch along the drawn line and then trim the seam allowances to ¼". Flip the resulting corner triangle open. Press the seam allowances toward the corner. Stitch, trim, and press a marked square to the other end of the same rectangle to make a flying-geese unit.

APPLIQUÉ

Typically for appliqué, the instructions specify to *not* add a seam allowance around the shapes that you cut from template plastic, freezer paper, or fusible web. For the patterns in this book, however, you will need to add a seam allowance along the straight outer edges of any shapes that will be sewn into the block's outer seam allowance. These are noted on the pattern pages, so follow the instructions carefully.

For detailed instructions on needle-turn, freezer-paper, and fusible appliqué methods, you can find free information online at ShopMartingale.com/HowtoQuilt.

MAKING PATCHWORK TEMPLATES

Most quilters prefer to rotary cut their patchwork pieces, but some shapes, especially in elongated rectangular blocks, are difficult to cut this way and require a cutting template.

To make a template, trace the shape from the book page onto template plastic. These shapes include the ¼" seam allowance. Use a ruler to mark accurate and straight cutting lines. Then cut out the template on the marked lines using a scissors or a rotary cutter and ruler. Be sure to transfer any grainline arrows or other information to the template. You may find it helpful to use an awl or the point of your seam ripper to make small holes at the corners where the seamlines intersect.

Then trace around the template onto the fabric, paying attention to the grainline. Cut out each fabric shape on the marked lines. Mark the seamline intersections through the small holes for easier matching of starting and stopping points for sewing seams.

Block 12 • String Star
Block directions on page 21.

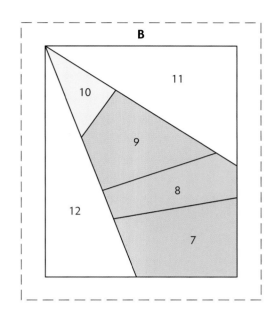

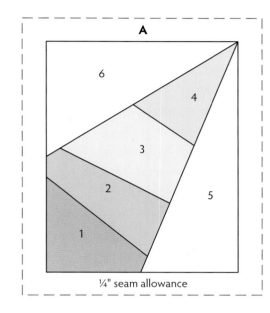

¼" seam allowance

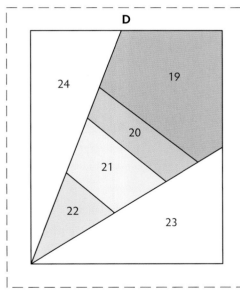

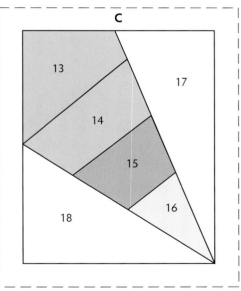

Block 23 • Clamshell
Block directions on page 32.

Block 21 • This-a-Way
Block directions on page 30.

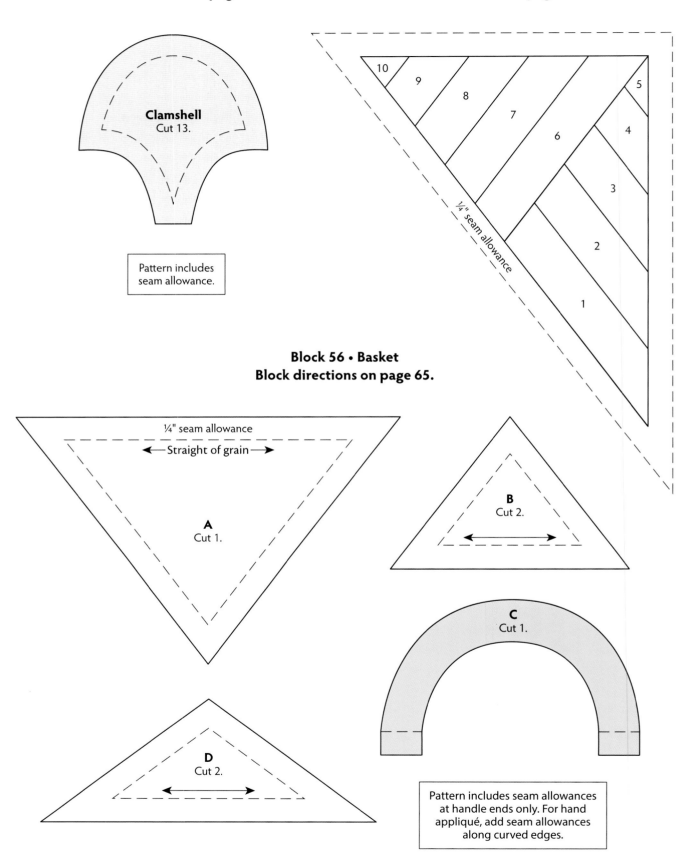

Clamshell
Cut 13.

Pattern includes
seam allowance.

¼" seam allowance

10
9
8
7
6
5
4
3
2
1

Block 56 • Basket
Block directions on page 65.

¼" seam allowance
←—Straight of grain—→

A
Cut 1.

B
Cut 2.

C
Cut 1.

D
Cut 2.

Pattern includes seam allowances
at handle ends only. For hand
appliqué, add seam allowances
along curved edges.

Block 73 • Water Wheel
Block directions on page 82.

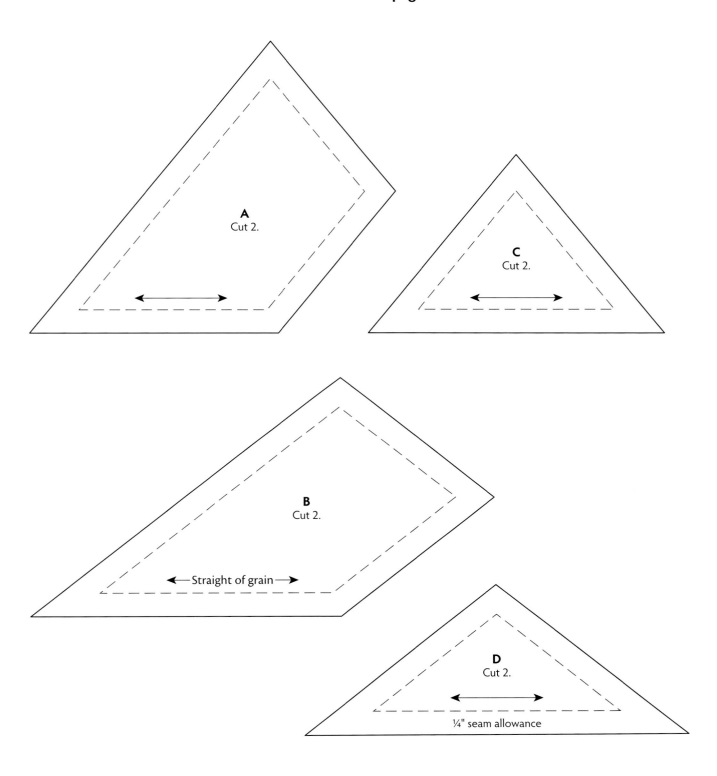

A
Cut 2.

C
Cut 2.

B
Cut 2.

← Straight of grain →

D
Cut 2.

¼" seam allowance

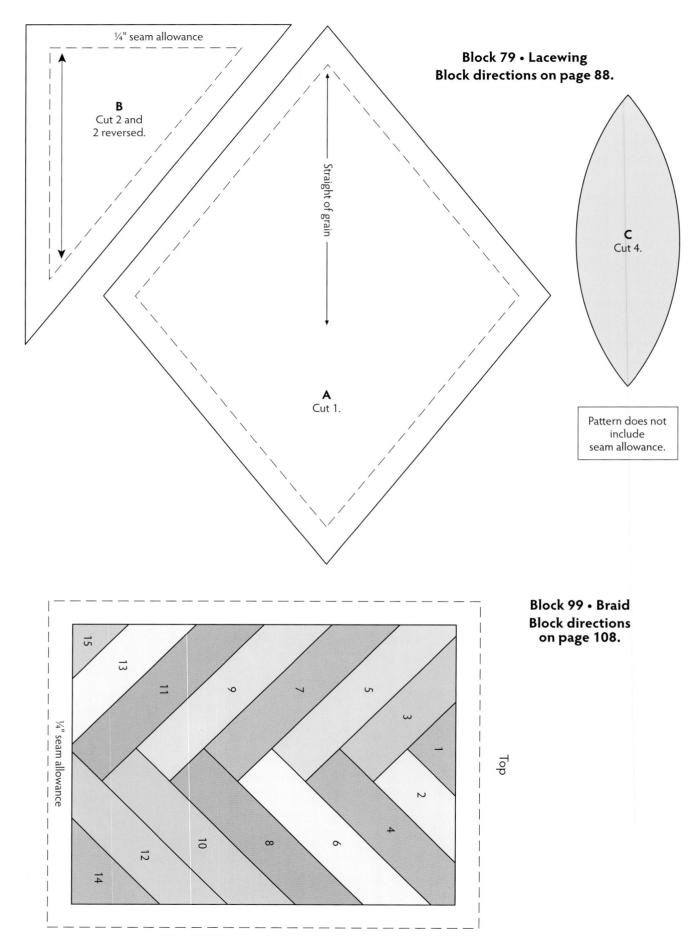

¼" seam allowance

B
Cut 2 and
2 reversed.

Straight of grain

A
Cut 1.

Block 79 • Lacewing
Block directions on page 88.

C
Cut 4.

Pattern does not
include
seam allowance.

Block 99 • Braid
**Block directions
on page 108.**

¼" seam allowance

Top

15
13
11
9
7
5
3
1
2
4
6
8
10
12
14

Block 90 • Slant
Block directions on page 99.

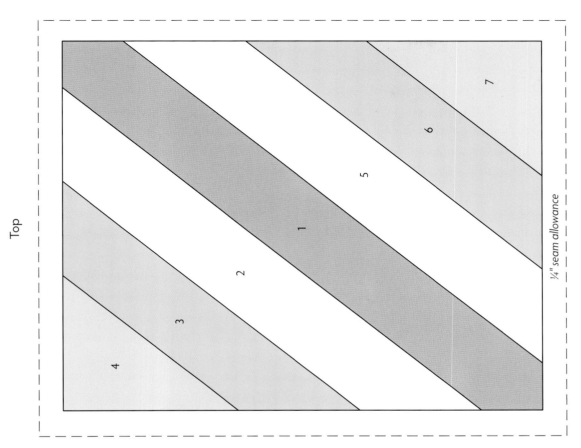

Block 136 • Comforter
Block directions on page 145.

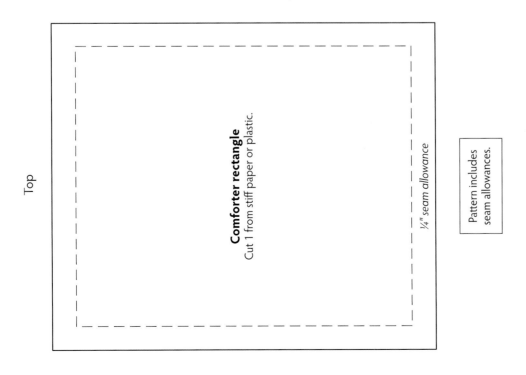

Block 116 • Love Letter
Block directions on page 125.

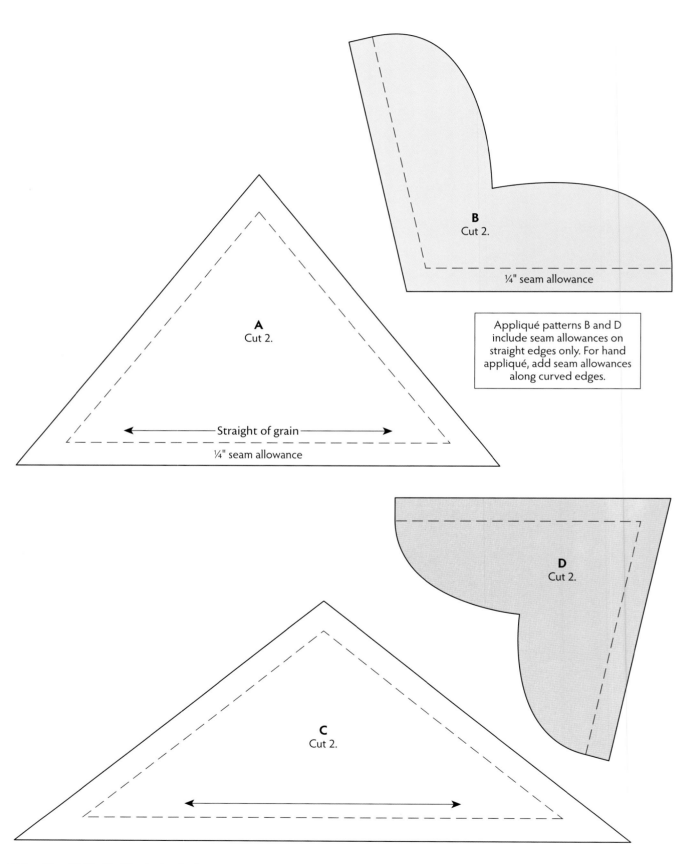

B
Cut 2.

¼" seam allowance

Appliqué patterns B and D
include seam allowances on
straight edges only. For hand
appliqué, add seam allowances
along curved edges.

A
Cut 2.

←———————— Straight of grain ————————→

¼" seam allowance

D
Cut 2.

C
Cut 2.

Block 120 • Tree
Block directions
on page 129.

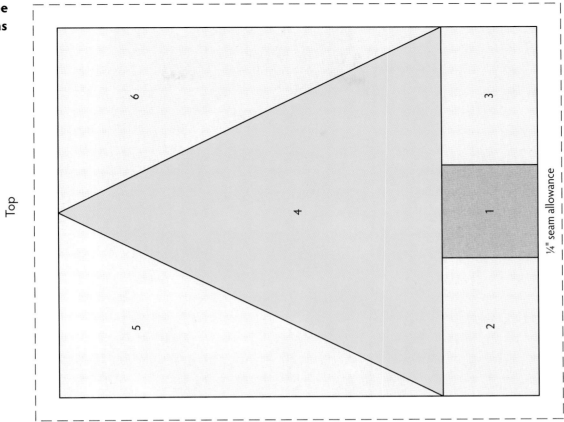

Top

¼" seam allowance

Block 145 •
Stairwell
Block directions
on page 154.

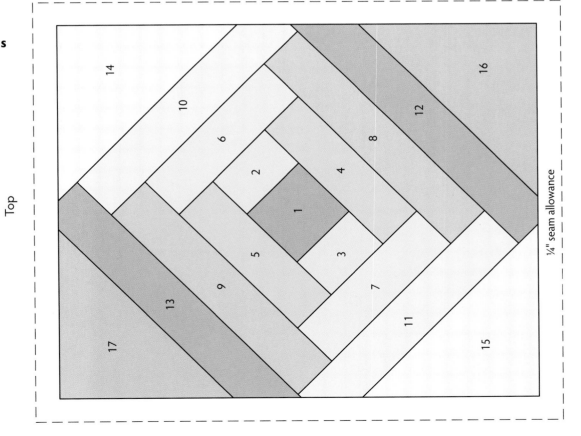

Top

¼" seam allowance

Block 157• Rafters
Block directions on page 166.

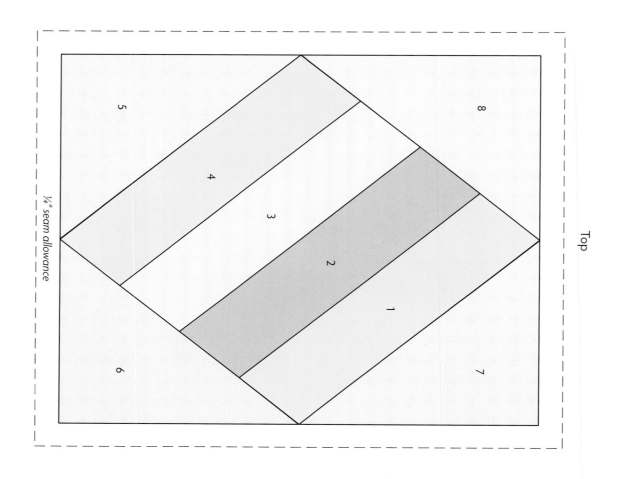

Block 163 • Flight
Block directions on page 172.

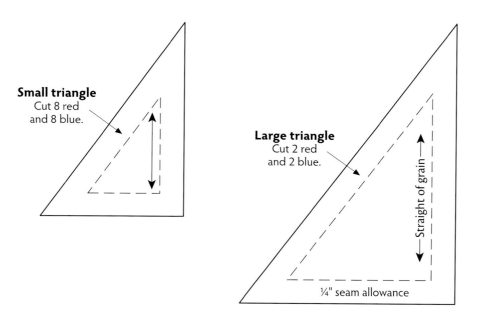

Block 167• Crazy
Block directions on page 176.

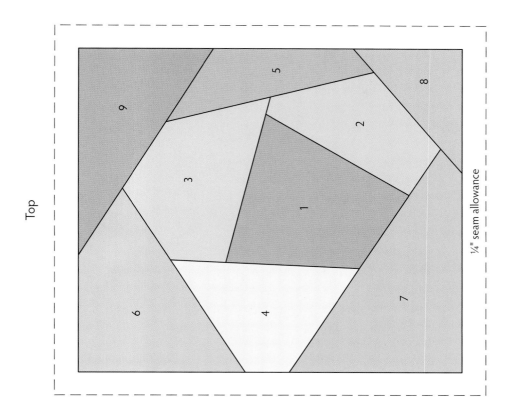

Block 182 • Signature
Block directions on page 191.

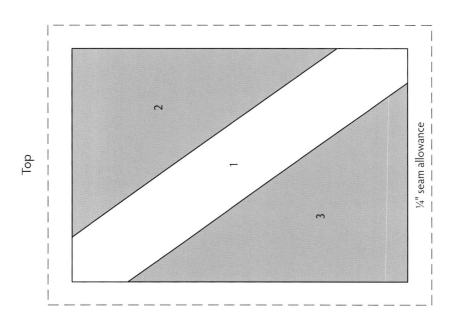

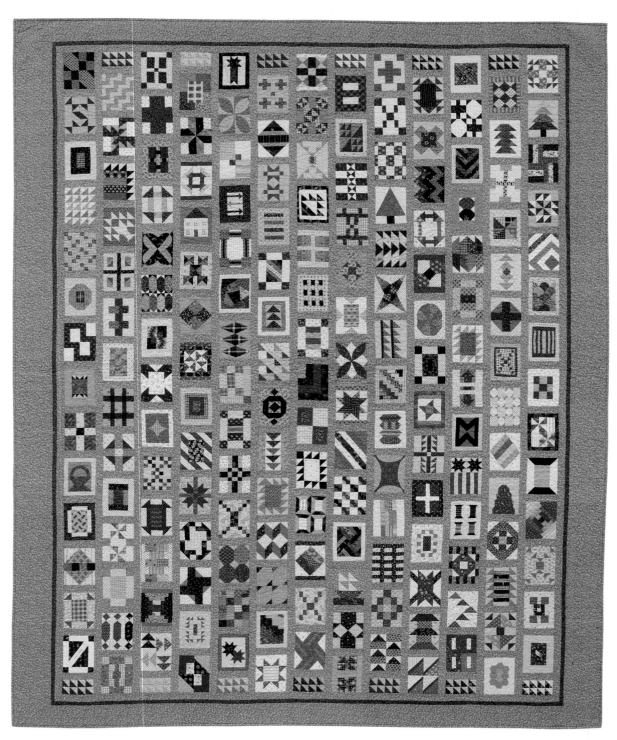

The Sparrow's Window

Pieced by Linda M. Koenig and quilted by Viki Kirby.
See layout key on page 203.

Finished quilt size: 77½" × 93½"

61	150	122	128	123	91	124	114	85	13	129	136	131
65	121	151	132	125	133	148	163	127	95	135	98	137
149	96	130	100	97	105	93	94	101	102	99	103	139
25	108	107	106	104	109	154	71	120	5	119	146	138
166	117	116	110	63	118	168	19	11	66	4	111	140
171	165	64	62	167	74	67	20	12	161	6	112	23
55	172	164	181	169	75	68	79	134	160	80	113	142
57	60	173	174	180	31	70	22	15	159	8	155	143
58	152	40	170	34	32	92	90	16	46	9	157	156
56	48	39	37	35	33	72	30	14	87	10	158	147
17	49	38	78	77	76	89	21	54	86	7	3	145
59	50	41	42	36	178	176	141	18	126	81	2	144
53	51	162	44	43	179	177	24	88	84	82	1	153
182	27	47	28	45	29	73	26	175	52	83	69	115

Above is a layout key for The Sparrow's Window, opposite. The numbers correspond to the 182 blocks in this book. Each vertical row contains 14 blocks, one half block that finishes to 2" × 4" (made with eight half-square-triangle units that finish to 1"), and 14 sashing rectangles. Sashing strips separate the rows; the quilt is framed with inner, middle, and outer borders.

To make the quilt shown, stitch 182 blocks and 13 half blocks, and then cut the following pieces for sashing and borders:

+ 182 blue sashing rectangles, 1½" × 4½"
+ 14 blue sashing strips, 1½" × 84½"
+ 2 blue inner-border strips (top and bottom edges), 1½" × 66½"
+ 2 navy middle-border strips (side edges), 1" × 86½"
+ 2 navy middle-border strips (top and bottom edges), 1" × 67½"
+ 2 blue outer-border strips (side edges), 5½" × 87½"
+ 2 blue outer-border strips (top and bottom edges), 3½" × 77½"

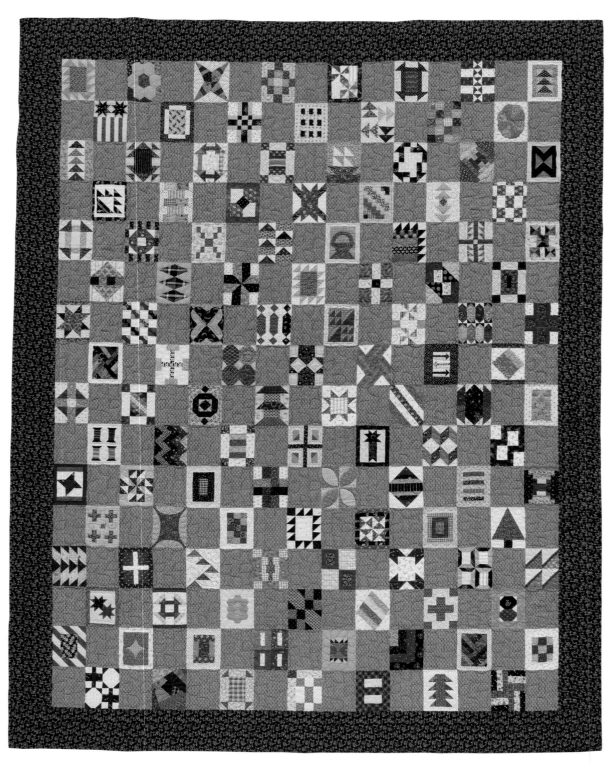

It's Not Square
Pieced by Carol Hopkins and quilted by Lisa Ramsey

Finished quilt size: 70" × 90"

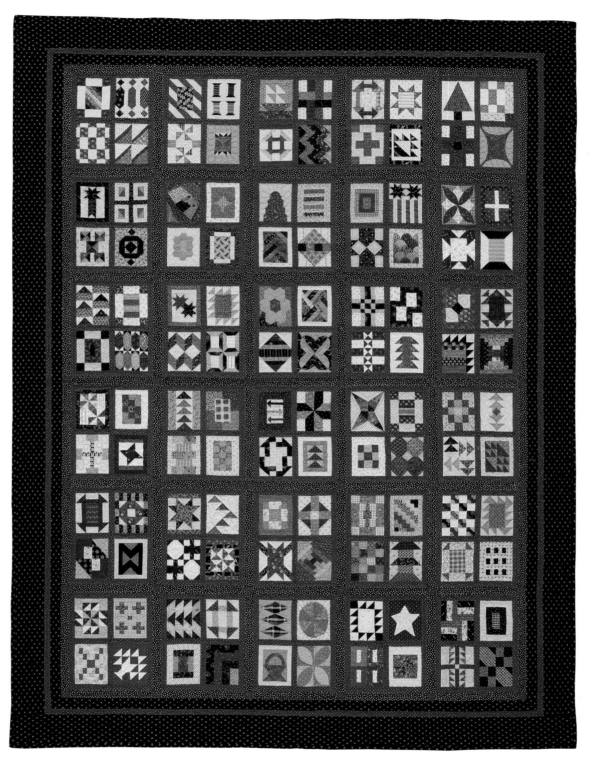

Close to My Heart

Pieced by Pam Antalis and quilted by Lisa Ramsey

Finished quilt size: 68½" × 84"

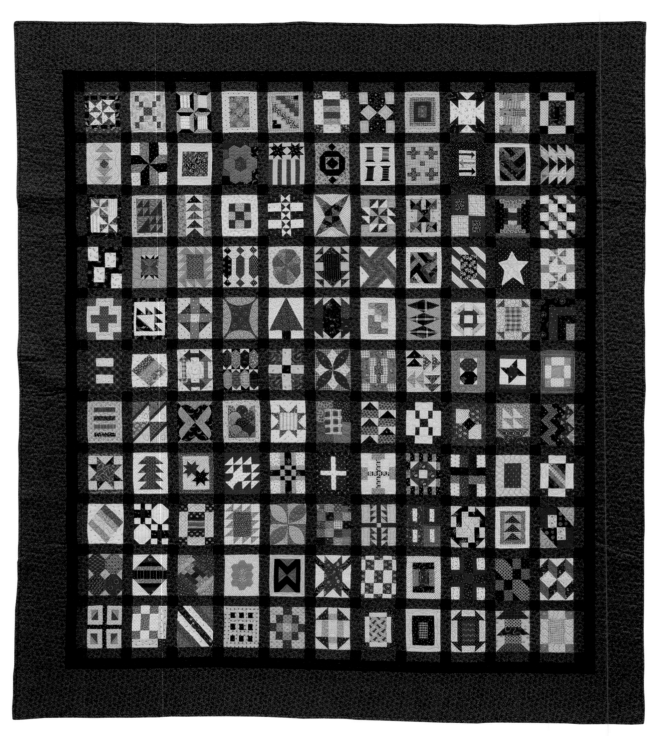

Small Town Parade

Pieced by Garnet Roesel and
quilted by Lisa Ramsey

Finished quilt size: 71" × 82"

Precious Metals

Pieced by Judy Barmann and
quilted by Theresa Cantwell

Finished quilt size: 35" × 40"

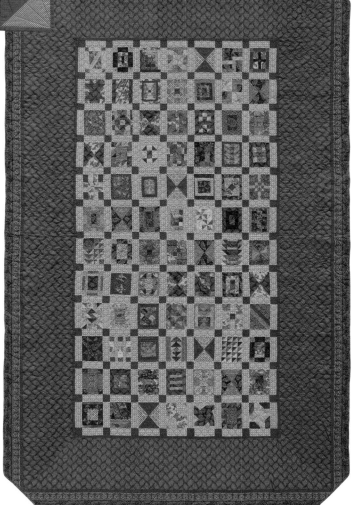

Xtra Inch × Inch

Pieced by Xenia Cord and
quilted by Ed Fennell

Finished quilt size: 67" × 103"

Acknowledgments

Thank you to Jennifer Keltner, Karen Soltys, and Karen Burns for seeing potential in a pile of quilt blocks and working with us and your talented Martingale staff to document them in this book.

We are ever grateful for our Lafayette quilting friends, Garnet Roesel and Pam Antalis, and North Stars members Theresa Arnold, Judy Barmann, Xenia Cord, Ruth Pedigo, Mary Jane Teeters-Eichacker, and Cec Purciful, who contributed their quilting talents, time, and moral support to the 4" × 5" block exchange and challenge that created the unique blocks and finished quilts for this book.

We wouldn't even have finished quilts to showcase in the photo gallery if it weren't for our gifted machine quilters, Theresa Cantwell, Ed Fennell, Lisa Ramsey, and Viki Kirby. We are always amazed by your creative designs and thankful for your willingness to help us meet deadlines.

And last, but never least, we thank our husbands and children for their support and patience as we embark on quilting adventures like writing this book.

About the Authors

Carol Hopkins lives with her husband, Edward, and her 36-year-old (and counting) fabric stash in West Lafayette, Indiana. Her favorite moments are those spent with her three children, their spouses, and her grandchildren, two of whom recently made their first quilts and pillowcases. She has published three best-selling *Civil War Legacies* books with Martingale, and created more than 100 individual quilt patterns marketed as "Civil War Legacies" and "Vintage Legacies" for her company, Carol Hopkins Designs. She is known for her scrappy, pieced-quilt designs, each of which includes dozens of 18th- or 19th-century reproduction fabrics. Carol's patterns are sold worldwide, and many of her designs have been featured in national and international quilt magazines. To learn more about Carol and see further examples of her work, visit CarolHopkinsDesigns.com.

Linda M. Koenig passed away shortly before this book went to press, saddening all of us who worked with her. Despite being ill, Linda put great effort into making this book a superb resource for lovers of reproduction fabrics and seekers of both classic and unusual block patterns, and we're grateful that she did.

A talented quilter, Linda made antique-inspired scrap quilts for more than 30 years. Her impressive quilts appeared in both periodicals and books, and for nine years she owned an Indianapolis quilt shop, where she shared her expertise in workshops on reproducing antique scrap quilts. Martingale is honored to share Linda's legacy of creative, inspiring quiltmaking through *The 4" × 5" Quilt-Block Anthology*.